Learning Through Movement in the K-6 Classroom

This book offers a creative and practical guide for K-6 teachers on how to effectively integrate movement into the curriculum to increase student engagement, deepen learning, improve retention, and get kids moving during the school day.

Chapters offer concrete ideas for integrating creative movement and theater into subjects such as math, science, literacy, and social studies. Drawing on two decades of experience, Dr. Becker outlines key skills, offers rich examples, and provides adaptable and flexible classroom tested lesson plans that align with Common Core Standards, the NGSS, C3 Social Studies Standards, and the National Core Arts Standards. Activities are grounded in arts integration, which is steadily gaining interest in school reform as an effective teaching strategy that increases student outcomes academically and socially—particularly effective for students who have traditionally been marginalized.

This book will benefit practicing educators who want to invigorate their practice, preservice teachers who want to expand their toolkit, and school leaders looking to employ policies that support movement and arts during the school day. Jump in and get your kids *Learning Through Movement* and see how active and engaging learning can be!

Kelly Mancini Becker, Ed.D, is an educator, researcher, and performing artist, currently teaching preservice teachers at The University of Vermont, USA, how to integrate the arts into classroom instruction. She provides professional development for schools, coaching for inservice teachers, and curriculum for arts integrated programming.

Also Available from Routledge Eye On Education
www.routledge.com/k-12

Drama for the Inclusive Classroom
Activities to Support Curriculum and Social-Emotional Learning
Sally Bailey

A Sensory Approach to K-6 STEAM Integration
Creative Materials-Based Units for Teachers
Kerry P. Holmes, Jerilou J. Moore, and Stacy V. Holmes

Joyful Learning
Tools to Infuse Your 6-12 Classroom with Meaning, Relevance, and Fun
Stephanie Farley

STEAM Teaching and Learning Through Arts and Design
A Practical Guide for PK-12 Educators
Debrah C. Sickler-Voigt

Learning Through Movement in the K-6 Classroom

Integrating Theater and Dance to Achieve Educational Equity

Kelly Mancini Becker

Routledge
Taylor & Francis Group

NEW YORK AND LONDON

Designed cover image: © Nurto Hassan

First published 2023
by Routledge
605 Third Avenue, New York, NY 10158

and by Routledge
4 Park Square, Milton Park, Abingdon, Oxon, OX14 4RN

Routledge is an imprint of the Taylor & Francis Group, an informa business

© 2023 Kelly Mancini Becker

ISBN: 978-1-032-28327-2 (hbk)
ISBN: 978-1-032-28325-8 (pbk)
ISBN: 978-1-003-29631-7 (ebk)

DOI: 10.4324/9781003296317

Typeset in Optima
by KnowledgeWorks Global Ltd.

For my mom and dad who encouraged me to go on stage in the first place, for my daughters who were always in the front row, for my friends who supported me from the wings, and for all the students I have worked with over the years who allowed me the chance to see them shine center stage (with lots of singing, dancing, and laughing along the way).

Contents

Contents

Contents

Introduction
Let's Get This Moving!

Picture This .... The Body as Integral to Learning

In a fifth-grade class a few years back, something remarkable happened that changed my perception of teaching and learning. It set me on a path to ensure that all students are valued for the skills and talents they bring to the classroom and to consider the importance of the body (not just the brain) in learning. While teaching a lesson in a fourth-grade classroom, I made a connection to Martin Luther King Jr. and the Civil Rights Movement. Out of the corner of my eye, I saw a student raise his fist in the air mimicking the sign of Black power. This student was making a connection to an arts-integrated lesson I had taught a few weeks prior. In that lesson, students entered the classroom to find photographs strewn across the floor from marches and protests of the Civil Rights Movement in the 1960s. While music from the period played, some spirituals and others protest songs, students were asked to explore the photos on the ground. They were invited to walk around taking some time to view the photographs and to see which ones "drew them in" or sparked their curiosity. After some time, students were invited to choose a photo that they found engaging and take a closer look. They were encouraged to look for "movement" in the picture, be it a person in the photograph making a motion (like marching) or a motion that might encapsulate a feeling expressed in the photo (like strength). The students were then asked to mimic or create three movements based on this exploration of the photograph that would be used as a building block for a movement exercise. This student chose a photograph depicting members

DOI: 10.4324/9781003296317-1

of the Black Panthers and the movement he chose was a raised fist in the air. Students used their movements in an activity called **diamonds** where they worked in groups of four and took turns leading and following while moving to music from the Civil Rights Movement (see *diamonds* lesson plan in Chapter 2). When this student raised his fists in the air, the other students followed. When his classmates took the lead, they shared their movements such as marching, holding up signs, and covering their eyes. The result was a riveting, emotionally charged experience for both mover and observer, and a powerful work of art that created a platform for a deep conversation about the impact of the Civil Rights Movement and the power of the people to make change through peaceful protest.

Having this student make this physical response to this lesson a few weeks later was pretty remarkable. This particular student struggled greatly in school. He was not engaged and rarely contributed to class discussions. This student was, however, completely engaged in the arts-integrated lesson with the photographs, and when this student demonstrated the raised fist gesture weeks later, I knew that he was making a connection to the pre-vious lesson. It was a sign that the lesson had not only been memorable for him, but he had internalized it in some way. Had I not been aware of the connection between the mind and body as a source of learning, I might have missed this student's contribution. Instead, I was able to acknowledge his connection to the material and congratulate him for his good "thinking."

Why was this moment in my teaching career so pivotal? It made me realize how many students disappear in the classroom landscape because we champion only certain ways of knowing, both how students access content and express what they know, ignoring the body in the process (Fattal, 2019). If we want to reach *all* of our students and help each of them grow, develop, and learn, we need to vary our teaching practices to welcome and acknowledge the variety of ways of knowing our students bring to the classroom.

There are a few key concepts that this teaching/learning episode espouses which will be covered in this chapter: the value of using the body as a means of learning (**embodied cognition**), how learning is deepened when we ask students to transfer information from one sign system to another (**transmediation**), the importance of **engagement** for student success, and the impact that integrating the arts (**art integration**) has on learning (see Figure 1.1). Most of all, this teaching episode demonstrates the value of integrating movement with content and the impact it has on student success, which will be the focus of this book.

Figure 1.1 Students are fully engaged in an arts integrated lesson where they are asked to create shapes using their bodies.
(Photo taken by author with permission from The Integrated Arts Academy [IAA])

Now Is the Time to Get Moving: Changing the Way We Teach and Learn to Improve Educational Outcomes for All Students

There are a multitude of reasons why now is the time to get kids up and moving to learn throughout the school day. Current research on the brain has shown that movement is vital for learning, growing brain cells in the areas where long-term memories are stored, improving retention, producing serotonin that helps students feel good about school, and improving physical and emotional well-being (Hardiman, 2012; Ratey, 2008; Rinne et al., 2011; Willis & Willis, 2020). Most children in the US are not getting the daily recommended amount of exercise during the day, so schools *stepping* it up in this area can have a major impact on student health (The National Office of Disease Prevention and Health Promotion, 2022). Integrating movement into learning can also better serve the growing population of students who are multilingual learners[1] (Snyder & Fenner, 2021) in the US public schools. It is reported that in 2019, there were 1 in 10 children, 4.8 million students in our schools for which English is not their first language (Kaplan, 2019). Integrating movement will more quickly bring students who are language learners into the community and advance their language acquisition (Cahnamann-Taylor & McGovern, 2021). Research has also shown that art-infused pedagogy improves educational outcomes for BIPOC students and students of lower SES status (Robinson, 2013). Considering the rapidly changing demographics of the US public schools, it is imperative that we alter our teaching practices to ensure success for all students.

While there are many benefits to integrating movement (specifically drama and dance) with the K-6 curriculum, many teacher education programs offer little instruction in these areas (Hunter-Doniger & Fox, 2020). Therefore, teachers may have little or no experience teaching in this way. If teachers have not done theater or dance themselves, they may not feel comfortable working in these mediums and, therefore, not include them in their practices. The good news is that some schools and teachers have started to provide movement breaks during the school day often in the form of videos like *Go Noodle*. While these are helpful, this book will help you integrate movement with your content which has many more benefits for your students. Since there can be many competing demands on teachers to meet a variety of learning targets, integrating movement with the core content can make the best use of limited time. Most of all, this type of learning is FUN for both you and your students which makes everyone more excited to come to school.

This book is the result of over two decades of work done with students of all ages using movement be it theater or dance to improve educational outcomes. I have been a theater artist, a drama and music teacher in both public and private elementary schools, an arts integration specialist for schools, and a teaching artist for arts organizations. I currently teach on the college level in a teacher preparation program where I guide preservice teachers to use the arts as a vehicle for learning. All of the lessons shared in this book were tested with students in a variety of settings and are proven to be effective. Also included in this book are foundation skills, key concepts, and lessons learned that will support your efforts to integrate movement effectively in your classroom.

Shout Out to the Teachers, Students, and Theater Artists Who Have *Moved* Me Forward

As any theater artist will attest, many of the theater games we all use and teach have been passed around forever! It would be almost impossible to find the source for many of the activities shared in this book. It's like the game of telephone. You learn a theater game at a workshop, then you change it a bit to suit your needs and pass it on. Often, it is hard to know what the original game even looked like. I do, however, want to acknowledge a few of the pivotal sources upon which this work is built. Probably the most influential work of theater games is from Viola Spolin's *Improvisation for the Theater* (1963). Most theater teachers use this as their bible. I also worked with three arts organizations that shared many of their resources and ideas and helped me develop my skills: The Folger Shakespeare Library, The Shakespeare Theater, and The Center for Inspired Teaching. Many of the activities shared in this book were created in conjunction with these amazing organizations.

I also want to thank many teachers who have either invited me into their classrooms or taught me how to be a better teacher. I started as a teaching artist who leaned more toward the arts than teaching. Watching excellent teachers in action over the years has helped me understand how a classroom functions. Therefore, the games and activities in this book take management, classroom space, and school needs into consideration. Be assured that these activities were not developed in a bubble, but in real classrooms with all the joys and excitement as well as real constraints of learning in schools today.

I also want to thank the students I have had the pleasure to work with. Each encounter has improved my skills and helped shape these activities. I am grateful for all the laughs, ideas shared, insights, and amazing work that has shown me why this work is so important. All of the photographs in the book are from my years of working with students. Finally, I want to especially thank The Integrated Arts Academy (students, teachers, and principal) in Burlington, VT, for allowing me to recently conduct an artist in residency where I collected both stories and photographs that are present throughout the book.

What You Will Find in This Book

In this book, you will find all the support you need to get kids *Learning Through Movement*. It will help build your skills in a variety of areas that support this type of teaching and learning. Stories are shared from the field about how these activities play out in classrooms as well as rationale for integrating movement into each subject area: math, science, literacy, and social studies (see Figure 1.2 students using movement in a literacy class). The core of this book is classroom-tested lesson plans that you can integrate into a variety of content areas (lessons that are aligned with standards and found in typical elementary curriculum). These lesson plans begin with a short explanation, so you can quickly decide if the lesson is right for your class. There is no need to read this book in order, simply go to the subject area that you are in need of invigorating and start there. So, let's get *moving* on this and get kids out of their seats and on their feet to learn!

Why Get Kids Learning Through Movement?

Start with Students' Health and Well-Being

As the last few years have taught us, schools have to consider the health and well-being of their students first and foremost. We know this is foundational

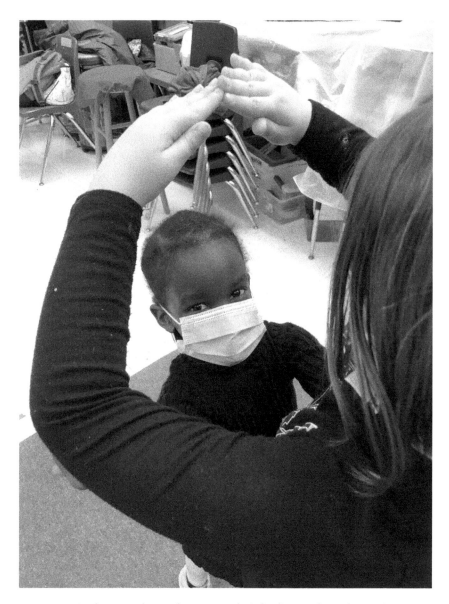

Figure 1.2 Students work together to use their bodies to shape letters in an arts integrated literacy lesson.
(Photo taken by author with permission from IAA)

to any learning. Integrating movement into the learning that occurs during the school day has many benefits for our school-age children. It provides students a chance to move more often during the school day which is important for children's growing bodies and minds. Movement provides students with an opportunity to take a quick break, get their wiggles out, reenergize with breath, and get some blood flowing through the body and to the brain. Research done by Lengel and Kuczala (2010) proved that if the body is inactive for more than 20 minutes, there is decline in neural communication. Finding ways to get kids up and moving often during the school day while learning content saves valuable time and helps students' brains stay active and primed for learning.

Getting students up and moving to learn during the school day may also help to combat the rising childhood obesity rates in the US. According to the US Office of Disease Prevention and Health Promotion, adolescent children are not getting enough physical activity each day, with only one in five adolescents in the US meeting physical activity guidelines for aerobic and muscle-strengthening activities (The National Office of Disease Prevention and Health Promotion, 2022). Childhood obesity has tripled in the last three decades with frightening statistics in the US with higher rates in African American and Hispanic communities (Ogden et al., 2014). In 2017-2020, obesity prevalence was 20.7% among 6- to 11-year-olds (Center for Disease Control and Prevention [CDC], 2023). Diminishing recesses and physical education during the school day, biproducts of more time devoted to preparing for standardized tests, will result in even greater sedimentary school hours. This makes the need for students to get on their feet and moving even more critical.

The US Department of Health and Human Services has developed clear guidelines for school-age children which includes 60 minutes a day of moderate to rigorous physical activity which should include "opportunities [...] that are enjoyable and that offer variety" (The U.S. Department of Health and Human Services, 2018, p. 48). The report also highlights the benefits of physical activity for brain health for children ages 6–13 which includes improved cognition (memory, processing speed, executive function, and academic achievement in test taking) (p. 40). They also report on the risk factors associated with a sedimentary lifestyle and too much sitting. Despite all we know about the importance of less sitting and more moving, the school day is still dominated by sitting activities.

Physical activity is also good for children's well-being. Teachers on all levels of education have affirmed that the past two years of the pandemic have done more than just put children behind in their learning, it has also taken a toll on their mental health. There has been a notable increase in attention to students' social-emotional learning (SEL) during the school day to help to address students' current needs. Physical activity during the school day could support student's well-being as it has been proven to help reduce the risk of depression in children ages 6–17 (The U.S. Department of Health and Human Services, 2018). Movement increases serotonin and dopamine in the brain which helps improve mood (Hardiman, 2012; Ratey, 2008). Movement-centered activities such as dance and theater also often require collaboration among students offering more time to work with their peers which has proven to support their social emotional well-being (Sprenger, 2020). Such activities can also improve self-efficacy, often providing opportunities for students who have alternative talents not always captured in traditional methods to shine (Goldberg, 2021). Most importantly, activities that engage the body such as dance and theater often produce joy and laughter (which is not only much needed), but neuroscience has shown positively impacts learning (Hardiman, 2012).

Movement and the Brain: What We Can Learn from Neuroscience

There is mounting evidence of the positive effects of physical activity on student learning. Movement helps students focus and perform better in academic arenas, improves memory, and increases retention (Hardiman, 2012; Ratey, 2008; Rinne et al., 2011; Willis & Willis, 2020). John J. Ratey (2008), in his pivotal book *SPARK: The Revolutionary New Science of Exercise and the Brain*, literally got us all *moving* in the right direction. He found that daily morning exercise improved brain function, memory, attention, and mood of students. Ratey states: "Moving our muscles produces proteins that travel through the bloodstream and into the brain, where they play pivotal roles in the mechanisms of our highest thought processes" (p. 5). Ratey documented multiple case studies where entire school districts that adopted rigorous daily exercise programs showed dramatically improved test scores. Movement has been shown to grow new brain cells, many of which are located in the hippocampus, the part of the brain that is essential for long-term memory function. Movement also acts to stimulate the brain-derived neurotrophic factor (BDNF), which supports the growth, maturation, and survival of neurons in the nervous system (Hernandez, 2018). BDNF stimulates growth of new neurons, supports brain plasticity, and improves function which is essential for learning and memory (Bathina & Das, 2015). Willis and Willis (2020) share that movement is associated with increased release of dopamine in the brain which has many benefits for students. She suggests that integrating movement in the learning process is a great way to "ignite" students' learning.

Integrating physical movement into a lesson has also been shown to increase retention (Hardiman, 2012; Hardiman et. al, 2019). Think back to your time in school. It is likely the time you spent acting out a scene from a play in a literacy class or dissecting a frog in science that you remember most. Hardiman's (2012) research shows that the more ways in which we receive information, the greater the potential is for retention. Rae Pica (2012) in her book *Experiences with Movement and Music* shares from Fauth (1990, p. 160) that we retain only 10% of what we read and 20% of what we hear. However, we retain "90% of what we hear, see, say, and do (acting out, dramatizing, dancing, painting, drawing, and constructing)" (p. 12). As Lengel and Kuczala (2010) argue in *The Kinesthetic Classroom: Teaching and Learning through Movement* during the school day "provides the opportunity for students to grow cognitively, physically, mentally, emotionally, and socially" (p. 2).

Embodied Cognition: Connection of Mind and Body in Learning

The notion that the body and mind are connected and that the body is integral to brain function is a burgeoning field of study called *embodied cognition* with research emerging from linguists, philosophers, and cognitive scientists (Fadjo et al., 2009; Shapiro & Stolz, 2019). Using movement in the teaching and learning of content is also gaining attention in educational research (Johnson-Glenberg et al., 2014; Petrick Smith et al., 2014) and may provide insights into how engaging the body may support student learning. Hardiman (2012) in her research-based *Brain Targeted Teaching Model* identifies essential elements for student learning based on the newest brain research including connecting to students' emotions, providing novelty, and fostering creativity through the use of the visual arts, music, and movement.

Glenberg (1997) developed one of the first theories regarding embodied cognition. His work in the late 1990s with the Laboratory of Embodied Cognition focused on ways perception and action could influence language comprehension. Glenberg (2015) argued that there was a link between memory and embodiment and that our perceptions are influenced by our physical reactions in the world:

> Human thinking is [not] computer-like. Instead, as with all animals, our thoughts are based on bodily experiences, and our thoughts and behaviors are controlled by bodily and neural systems of perception, action, and emotion interacting with the physical and social environments. We are embodied; nothing more. Embodied cognition is about cognition formatted in sensorimotor experience, and sensorimotor systems make those thoughts dynamic. Even processes that seem abstract, such as language comprehension and goal understanding, are embodied. Thus, embodied cognition is not limited to 1 type of thought or another: It is cognition.
>
> (Glenberg, 2015, p. 165)

What Glenberg is affirming is that we learn using our bodies. Think of the tiniest child who uses their mouth, fingers, and toes to explore and understand the world. Why would these tools stop being useful once children enter the classroom door?

Brain research supports the mind-body connection (Moseley et al., 2013; Pulvermuller et al., 2001). Pulvermuller et al. (2001) did a seminal study where they used high-resolution electroencephalogram (EEG) recordings to test what happened in the brain and body of participants when action verbs were presented on a screen. They found that when action verbs associated with body functions in the face, legs, and arms were given, participants showed activity in the brain closest to the area of the brain that activates those parts of the body. For example, if the word "talk" was projected on the screen, the area of the brain that controls the face would show activation. This study marked a major shift in both the discussion and implications for embodied cognition. In a similar study, using more advanced brain activity equipment, Moseley et al. (2013) affirmed the finding that certain words activated specific parts of the brain. The researchers used a variety of words from action verbs to abstract words and found that the strongest associations were with action verbs such as "knead," "jog," and "chew" (p. 5). In a recent study, Neilsen et al. (2020) found that a pedagogy utilizing the arts "enhances the opportunities for learners to express, explore and possibly negotiate their identities in the classroom and can be a way to support them to gain more knowledge and access into their own embodied experiences, the experiences of others, the curriculum and the larger world" (p. 4).

Acting and Cognitive Function

Many of the activities in this book are grounded in theater, which greatly depends on the body (physicalization) and gesture for its expression. From the Greeks, who used exaggerated movements of the body and hands to emphasize emotions and vaudeville comedians that used gesture and large body movements to accentuate their physical comedy to slap-stick comedy in today's sitcoms, the use of the body is central to the art of acting. Some research that investigated what happens when actors learn lines might illuminate the role that movement has on memory and the learning process. Noice and Noice (2006), actors and psychologists, have spent 20 years studying acting and its connection to cognitive function and memory. They sought to reveal what functions help actors learn large amounts of dialogue quickly and with ease. After testing a variety of theories in various studies, they considered a technique actors use to emotionally connect with the text or attempt to feel what they are saying is true. Noice and Noice (2006) have coined this concept "active experiencing" (AE), which they define as the "use (of) all physical, mental, and emotional channels to communicate the meaning of material to another person, either actually present or imagined" (p. 15). This use of active experiencing improved participants' memory of a text (as well as speed and accuracy) in their study, with a measured 60% retention rate for participants using AE versus 50% retention rate for participants who used typical memorization techniques. This study was replicated in multiple settings and with varied populations and revealed similar results. Noice and Noice (2006) also investigated a concept of "subject-performed tasks" (SPT), which is the act of connecting short phrases of text such as "move the cup" or "lift the pen" while actually performing the task. This occurrence, asserts Noice and Noice, may be explained by the use of motoric codes, a belief that when learning information, some kind of "code" is created in the brain, be it a picture, verbal, or motion code.

Transmediation: Using a Multimodal Approach

Noice and Noice (2006), in their discussion of motoric codes and a transfer of an idea from one medium to another using a type of code, is closely aligned with the idea of transmediation. The term is grounded in the work of Charles Subor Pierce (1839–1914) and semiotics, the idea that meaning making can be made through sign systems other than language. Transmediation takes this notion one step further by demonstrating the value of translating from one system to another, for example, text to image, image to music, movement to text. Siegel (1995) has studied transmediation and its impact on learning with findings that support the use of arts in learning for its enacting of transmediation. She argues that schools are verbocentric, which means they privilege the written and spoken word as the primary mode of learning and ways of knowing, ignoring the other ways that humans make meaning such as with images, music, and movement. Siegel argues we need more than "words" to engage in generative and reflective thinking. Encouraging students to translate between two symbols systems, for example, asking students to take away key ideas from a reading or text and articulate those ideas in another format such as in painting or music, expands and heightens students' meaning-making, which is essential for learning (p. 456). Siegel (1995) describes how transmediation works:

> Consider what happens when learners draw their interpretations of a written text, whether a story or an expository piece. They must arrive at some understanding and then find some way to cross ("trans") the boundaries between language and art such that their understanding is represented pictorially; it is in the sense that one sign system is explored in terms of (mediation) another.
>
> (p. 461)

Language in both the written and spoken word still dominates the way educators both share key concepts and ask students to demonstrate their understandings. Many educators would argue that reading and writing are central to effective communication and should be central to teaching and learning. However, if this is the only way we present content or assess students' understanding, who is being left out? Fattal (2019) argues that privileging the written and spoken word limits communication channels in the classroom as well as leaving behind the growing population of students in our schools who are multilingual learners.

While there is limited research on the effects of transmediation on learning, there is some research that suggests its effectiveness. Albers (2006) suggests that a multimodal approach to curriculum design can positively impact learning in literacy, encouraging students to express more complex meanings. She argues that transmediation offers students more flexibility and choice in how they express their learning and is a powerful tool for training both inservice and preservice teachers. Goldberg (2021) does not use the term transmediation, but she acknowledges the value of this process. She calls it "translating through representation" when students translate and represent subject matter content through the arts (p. 50). Goldberg argues that this is closely linked to "thinking in metaphors" and is central to learning. Transmediation has gained little attention in educational research, but may be helpful in understanding the value of using the arts as a vehicle for learning.

Benefits of Arts Integration

Most of the activities in this book are grounded in the performing arts, specifically dance and theater. The performing arts are an excellent tool for integrating movement into the K-6 curriculum because movement is so integral to their processes. The concept of using the arts as a vehicle for learning is called **arts integration** (see Figure 1.3 as students demonstrate a star shape created in a dance and math integrated lesson). Donovan and Pascale (2022) in their book *Integrating the Arts Across the Curriculum* define arts integration as an "investigation of curricular content through artistic exploration. In this process, the arts provide an avenue for rigorous investigation, representation, expression, and reflection of both curricular content and the art itself" (p. 12). Arts integration has been shown to be an effective means for engaging all students in learning and improving student outcomes in both academic and social development (Bamford, 2009; Burnaford et al., 2007; Catterall, 2002; Deasy, 2002). Several studies claim that involvement in the arts positively effects students' academic achievement (Ruppert, 2006; Vaughn & Winner, 2000). Ruppert (2006), who examined a federal database of over 25,000 middle and high school

Figure 1.3 This is a picture of students collaborating to create shapes in an activity called *Math Dance,* a lesson that integrates dance with a lesson in math. (Photo taken by author with permission from IAA)

students found that students that had "high arts involvement" did better on standardized tests (p. 8). Another study found similar results, affirming that students at schools that had an arts focus and included arts integration practices along with professional development performed better on statewide tests (Scripp & Paradis, 2014). A recent empirical study, with a randomized control design, found that arts integrated instruction was as effective or better than conventional instruction for student retention of science content. which foregrounds its potential for the use of the arts in learning for long-term retention of core content (Hardiman, et. al, 2019).

Diversifying Our Teaching Methods to Better Serve Underserved Student Populations

Another reason to expand our current methods of instruction is to improve educational outcomes for students who have been traditionally marginalized. US schools recently reached a significant milestone with the number of students who are Black, Indigenous, or People of Color (BIPOC) surpassing the number of non-Hispanic white students for the first time in history (Maxwell, 2014). This change in demographics and concerns over "the achievement gap," between white students and BIPOC students (what is now more appropriately called the opportunity gap), signals an urgency to alter the way schools operate. As stated by Maxwell (2014), "The United States must vastly improve the educational outcomes for this new and diverse majority of American students, whose success is inextricably linked to the well-being of the nation" (p. 1). In Blackshear and Culp's (2022) new collection of case studies, they reveal that racism and white supremacy not only negatively impact Black students' access to equable learning in US schools, but also their physical education. They foreground the inequities that effect Black students' physical education such as racist teaching practices as well as access to playgrounds and recreational spaces. They urge educators to adopt new methods of instruction that challenge the deep-rooted beliefs about Black youth and empower them to succeed. Dena Simmons (2019) urges educators to utilize *culturally responsive teaching* (Gay, 2000) that is student-centered and empowers students by encouraging them to use their lived experiences, knowledge, and realities in their learning. She calls us to "celebrate the diversity of students and use what they bring to the classroom to guide instruction" and to work to ensure academic outcomes for those who have been marginalized. Donovan and Anderberg (2020) suggest that arts engagement can help educators achieve culturally responsive teaching as well as inclusive classrooms:

> The arts […] provide multiple ways for students to express themselves and their understanding of key content as well as the world around them. The arts provide an open door for students to share their authentic voice and their unique differences and contributions to the learning community. Inclusive classrooms include language, images, stories, and material that reflect diversity and perspectives for groups or cultures that have been historically underrepresented.
>
> (p. 34)

Johnny Saldaña, J. (1995), a leader in what he calls "multiethnic education" argues that using improvisation and drama in the classroom, for example, to stage folklore, is a way to meet the needs of BIPOC students. He argues that "Eurocentric curriculum and approaches to teaching are incompatible with the child of color's cultural background and conditioning" and that we must achieve educational equality, which requires change in curriculum, teacher beliefs, and teaching styles (p. 25).

There is also an increase in students of lower socio-economic status (SES) in the US schools, who traditionally fall behind academically compared to students from higher SES backgrounds (Maxwell, 2014; Mehan, 1992). The number of students who are ELs is also on the rise, with the projection that in 2050 34% of children in the US will be either immigrants themselves or the child of a parent who is an immigrant (Maxwell, 2014). Research has shown that schools that are rich in arts learning, such as the use of arts integration and drama, positively improve outcomes for students with lower SES and BIPOC students as well as students who are ELs (Brouillette et al., 2014; Greenfader & Brouillette, 2014; Robinson, 2013; Scripp and Paradis, 2014). This is why it is essential that we utilize practices that help *all* students succeed by infusing our practices with rich arts learning opportunities and movement!

Importance of Student Engagement

Test scores are only one predictor of how effective our schools are and may not be a good judge of how we are meeting the needs of our students. Lack of engagement may be a sign that our methods are not capturing the imaginations and attention of our students, distancing them from the learning process. Lack of engagement impacts learning and can ultimately lead to dropout (Yazzie-Mintz, 2010). Arts integration has been shown to increase engagement and motivation, both necessary to improve student performance (Brouillette, 2019). In an extensive study on engagement and arts learning, Smithrim and Upitis (2005) found that students were most engaged in subjects that encouraged visual-spatial, interpersonal, and bodily-kinesthetic modes of learning. As noted by Danuser and Sabetti (2001), the more the senses are simultaneously involved in a learning process, the more engaging the experience (p. 77). Miller and Bogatova (2018) in their mixed method—4-year study of the impact of integrating dance, music, visual arts, and drama into the existing elementary school curriculum—found that such practices had a significant impact on student engagement. They also reported positive outcomes related to quality of teaching, improved learning habits for students, and a high level of satisfaction for teachers.

How often do schools utilize alternative modes of instruction such as kinesthetic and visual-spatial or consider engagement as a predictor of an effective lesson? Despite research that shows the positive effects of alternative teaching methods, most teachers are continuing to use direct instruction in the classroom that espouses one mode of access to content and demonstration of learning (Hardiman, 2003; Smithrim & Upitis, 2005). Tony Wagner (2012), a leader in the field of innovation and education, has argued that the world has changed greatly, and yet our schools have not. He fears that our educational practices are not producing students who can think critically and creatively and communicate effectively in effort to become the kind of workers we need in the 21st century. Other leaders in the field such as Ken Robinson, Dennis Littky, and Daniel Pink argue that schools have to change the way we teach in this technically and visually stimulating new world in effort to keep our students engaged and develop the next level of creative thinkers who can solve the most complex world problems (Hardiman, 2003).

Maxine Greene (1995), a leading educational philosopher, articulates the importance of *"Releasing the Imagination"* for our schools and world and argues that the arts are essential for helping us all envision what our schools and world should be:

> The extent to which we grasp another's world depends on our existing ability to make poetic use of our imagination, to bring into being the "as if" world created by writers, painters, sculptors, filmmakers, choreographers and composers, and to be in some manner a participant in the artists' world reaching far back and ahead in time.
>
> (p. 4)

This book will help the students in your classrooms not only "release their imaginations," but act as choreographers and theater artists who can envision a new world through their creativity and creations. I hope this book helps you not only get your students up and *moving*, but *move* your students to engage more deeply in learning and with each other.

Book Overview

Chapter 2, "Getting Ready to Move", is all about getting you, your students, and your classroom ready to do this kind of instruction—to move the desks aside and get kids moving! Getting kids out of their seats can be scary for teachers. There is a fear that with freedom there will be chaos. However, once expectations and boundaries are set, students will understand how to act appropriately in this new setting. This chapter will offer some ideas for setting up the expectations in an active classroom with exercises for practicing these expectations and some ideas for getting students warmed up for doing this kind of learning.

Chapter 3, "Setting the Stage for Success", shares some of the skills and concepts that are foundational to the success of doing activities grounded in theater and dance. Basic theater skills like improvisation and theater games will be shared to build your skills in this area to prepare you to successfully implement all the activities shared in this book.

Chapter 4, "Leaping for Literacy", encompasses a plethora of lessons that utilize movement in the teaching of language arts. The chapter begins with some rational and supporting research that demonstrates how movement and arts integration can improve literacy skills as well as be more inclusive for the range of linguistic abilities you may have in your classroom. Lessons include some work with poetry, action verbs, and how to stage a read-aloud or fable.

Chapters 5 and 6 address *math and science*. These two chapters demonstrate what a powerful tool theater and movement is for teaching math and science. The key argument made in these two chapters is that the use of movement (with special attention to gesture) in the instruction of math and science helps students better grasp complex concepts that often occur in these two subject areas. These two chapters are meant to open your eyes to the opportunities that await you and your students when you embrace what movement and the arts can bring to your STEM subjects. There is a reason that STEAM (Stem + the Arts) is gaining some traction in education.

Chapter 7, "Moving through History", is focused on using the performing arts, movement and dance to engage in social studies. Social studies content is one of the best subjects to integrate with the arts. Theater is about "living" in a character and a time period, so it is an excellent tool for engaging students in historical events. This chapter includes many ideas to enliven and deepen the learning in social studies.

Chapter 8 focuses on *assessment*. The arts are often deemed as extras or "fun" time, and therefore, not often assessed. However, assessing student progress in the arts is key to their success as well as students' development. Additionally, using the arts can offer you a chance to diversify your assessment tools. This chapter offers some new ways of thinking about and framing assessment centering the arts and some suggestions for making assessment more authentic and informative for both students and teachers.

Conclusion

The positive outcomes of using movement, specifically theater and dance, in the classroom to teach core subjects are extensive including greater retention, increased student engagement, deeper learning, as well as contributing to both the health and well-being of your students. Brain research supports both the connection of movement to greater brain health and improved learning. Students need more opportunities to get the recommended amount of physical activity each day. Since schools make up a large portion of that day, integrating movement with the teaching of core subjects is a great way to maximize precious learning time. It has been shown that arts learning improves educational outcomes for traditionally marginalized students. If we want to achieve educational equity, we must change our teaching practice to better serve all students in our increasingly diverse schools. It is time to take advice from researchers and educators alike and get your kids *Learning through Movement in your K-6 classroom!*

Note

1 This nomenclature used to describe children who are developing their English language proficiency has changed frequently in both practice and research. Using one term throughout this book is complicated. Multilingual learners (MLs) is a more strengths- based terminology that is becoming more readily used. It has been defined as "students whose parent or guardian report speaking one or more languages other than English at home" (Snyder & Fenner, 2021). This may include a variety of types of language learners (dual language learners L2s) as well as English learners (ELs), the more common term used in research. ELs is defined the same as MLs, but students who fall into this category qualify for language support services. In most cases, I will use the terms which are outlined in the research I am

referencing. When possible, and if I know the context of the students for which I am discussing, I will use the term MLs to provide a more asset- based perspective.

References

Albers, P. (2006). Imagining the possibilities in multimodal curriculum design. *English Education*, *38*(2), 75–101. https://www.jstor.org/stable/40173215

Bamford, A. (2009). *The wow factor: Global research compendium on the impact of the arts in education* (2nd ed.). Waxmann.

Bathina, S., & Das, U. N. (2015) Brain-derived neurotrophic factor and its clinical implications. *Archives of Medical Science, 11*(6), 1164–1178. https://doi.org/10.5114/aoms.2015.56342

Blackshear, T. B., & Culp, B. (2022). *Critical race studies in physical education*. Human Kinetics.

Brouillette, L. (2019). *Arts integration in diverse K-5 classrooms: Cultivating literacy skills and conceptual understanding*. Teachers College Press.

Brouillette, L., Childress-Evans, K., Hinga, B., & Farkas, G. (2014). Increasing engagement and oral language skills of ELLs through the arts in the primary grades. *Journal for Learning Through the Arts, 10*(1). https://escholarship.org/uc/item/8573z1fm

Burnaford, G., Brown, S., Doherty, J., & McLaughlin, H. J. (2007). *Arts integration frameworks, research and practice: A literature review*. Arts Education Partnership.

Cahnamann-Taylor, M., & McGovern, K. R. (2021). *Enlivening instruction with drama and improv: A guide for second language and world language teachers*. Routledge.

Catterall, J. (2002). *The arts and the transfer of learning (Critical links: Learning in the arts and student academic and social development)* (pp. 151–157). Arts Education Partnership.

Center for Disease Control and Prevention (CDC). (2023). *Prevalence of childhood obesity in the United States*. Childhood Obesity Facts | Overweight & Obesity.

Danuser, E., & Sabetti, S. (2001). Energy pedagogy. In S. Sabetti, & L. Freligh (Eds.), *Life energy process* (pp. 75–92). Life Energy Media.

Deasy (2002). *Critical links: Learning in the arts and student academic and social development*. Arts Education Partnership.

Donovan, L., & Anderberg (2020). *Teacher as curator: Formative assessment and arts-based strategies*. Teachers College Press.

Donovan, L., & Pascale, L. (2022). *Integrating the arts across the curriculum* (2nd ed.). Shell Education.

Fadjo, C. L., Ming-Tsan, P. L., & Black, J. B. (2009). *Instructional embodiment and video game programming in an after school program*. Paper presented at the World Conference on Educational Multimedia, Hypermedia and Telecommunications, Chesapeake, VA.

Fattal, L. R. (2019). Transmediational practices in a bilingual elementary classroom. *NABE Journal of Research and Practice, 9*(2), 88–95. https://doi.org/10.1080/26390043.2019.1589295

Fauth, B. (1990). Linking the visual arts with drama, movement and dance for the young child. *Moving and learning for the young child* (pp. 159–187). American Alliance for Health, Physical Education, Recreation, and Dance.

Gay, G. (2000). *Culturally responsive teaching: Theory, research, and practice*. Teachers College Press.

Glenberg, A. M. (1997). What memory is for. *Behavioral and Brain Science, 20*, 1–55.

Glenberg, A. M. (2015). Few believe the world is flat: How embodiment is changing the scientific understanding of cognition. *Canadian Journal of Experimental Psychology, 69*(2), 165–171.

Goldberg, M. (2021). *Arts integration: Teaching subject matter through the arts in multicultural settings* (6th ed.). Routledge.

Greene, M. (1995). *Releasing the imagination: Essays on education, the arts, and social change*. Jossey-Bass Publishers.

Greenfader, C. M., & Brouillette, L. (2014). Boosting language skills of ELLs through dramatization and movement. *The Reading Teacher, 67*(3), 171–180.

Hardiman, M. (2003). *Connecting brain research with effective teaching: The brain-targeted teaching model*. Scarecrow Press.

Hardiman, M. (2012). *Brain targeted teaching model for 21st-century schools*. Corwin Press, Inc.

Hardiman, M., JohnBull, R. M., Carran, D. T., & Shelton, A. (2019). The effects of arts-integrated instruction on memory for science content. *Trends in Neuroscience and Education*, 14, 25–32.

Hernandez, K., (2018). *Activate: Deeper learning through movement, talk, and flexible classrooms*. Stenhouse Publishers. https://doi.org/10.3390/brainsci2040684

Hunter-Doniger, T., & Fox, M. (2020). Art connections: An investigation of art education courses for preservice generalists. *Arts Education Policy Review*, *121*(2), 55–62. https://doi.org/10.1080/10632913.2018.1530709

Johnson-Glenberg, M. C., Birchfield, D. A., Tolentino, L., & Koziupa, T. (2014). Collaborative embodied learning in mixed reality motion-capture environments: Two science studies. *Journal of Educational Psychology*, *106*(1), 86–104.

Kaplan, E. (2019). *6 essential strategies for teaching English language learners*. Edutopia. https://www.edutopia.org/article/6-essential-strategies-teaching-english-language-learners

Lengel, T., & Kuczala, M. (2010). *The kinesthetic classroom: Teaching and learning through movement*. Corwin.

Maxwell, L. (2014). U.S. school enrollment hits majority-minority milestone. *Education Week*, *34*(1), 1–2, 14, 15.

Mehan, H. (1992). Understanding inequality in schools: The contribution of interpretive studies. *Sociology of Education*, *65*(1), 1–20.

Miller, J. A., & Bogatova, T. (2018). Arts in education: The impact of the arts integration program and lessons learned. *Journal for Learning Through the Arts*, *14*(1). https://doi.org/10.21977/D914128357

Moseley, R. L., Pulvermuller, F., & Shtyrov, Y. (2013). Sensorimotor semantics on the spot: Brain activity dissociates between conceptual categories within 150ms. *Scientific Reports*, *3*, 1928). https://doi.org/doi:10.1038/srep01928

Neilsen, C. S., Samuel, G. M., Wilson, L., & Vedel, K. A. (2020). 'Seeing' and 'Being Seen': An embodied and culturally sensitive arts-integrated pedagogy creating enriched conditions for learning in multicultural schools. *International Journal of Education & the Arts*, *21*(2), 2–23. http://doi.org/10.26209/ijea21n2

Noice, H. & Noice, T. (2006). What studies of actors and acting can tell us about memory and cognitive functioning. *Current Directions in Psychological Science, 15*(1), 14–18.

Ogden, C., Carroll, M. D., Kit, B. K., & Flegal, K. M., (2014). Prevalence of childhood and adult obesity in the United States. *Journal of the American Medical Association, 311*(8), 806–814. https://doi.org/10.1001/jama.2014.732

Petrick Smith, C., King, B., & Hoyte, J. (2014). Learning angles through movement: Critical actions for developing understanding in an embodied activity. *The Journal of Mathematical Behavior, 36,* 95–108.

Pica, R. (2012). *Experiences in movement and music* (5th ed.). Cengage Learning.

Pulvermuller, F., Harle, M., & Hummel, F. (2001). Walking or talking? Behavioral and neurophysiological correlates of action verb processing. *Brain and Language, 78,* 143–168.

Ratey, J. J. (2008). *Spark: The revolutionary new science of exercise and the brain* (1st ed.). Little, Brown and Company.

Rinne, L., Gregory, E., Yarmolinskaya, J., & Hardiman, M. (2011). Why arts integration improves long-term retention of content. *International Mind, Brain, and Education, 5*(2), 89–96. https://doi-org.ezproxy.uvm.edu/10.1111/j.1751-228X.2011.01114.x

Robinson, A. H. (2013). Arts integration and the success of disadvantaged students: A research evaluation. *Arts Policy Review, 114*(4), 191–204.

Ruppert, S. (2006). *Critical evidence: How the arts benefit student achievement.* Arts Education Partnership.

Saldaña, J. (1995). *Drama of color: Improvisation with multiethnic folklore.* Heinemann.

Scripp, L., & Paradis, L. (2014). Embracing the burden of proof: New strategies for determining predictive links between arts integration teacher professional development, student arts learning, and student academic achievement outcomes. *Journal for Learning Through the Arts, 10*(1), 1–17. https://escholarship.org/uc/item/9ch5t8cw

Shapiro, L., & Stolz, S. A. (2019). Embodied cognition and its significance for education. *Theory and Research in Education, 17*(1), 19–39. https://doi.org/10.1177/1477878518822149

Siegel, M. (1995). More than words: The generative potential of transmediation for learning. *Canadian Journal of Education, 20*(4), 455–475.

Simmons, D. (2019). You can't be emotionally intelligent without being culturally response: Why FCS must employ both to meet the needs of our nation. *Journal of Family and Consumer Sciences, 111*(2), 7–16. https://doi.org/10.14307/JFCS111.2.7

Smithrim, K., & Upitis, R. (2005). Learning through the arts: Lessons of engagement. *Canadian Journal of Education, 28*(1/2), 109–127.

Spolin, V. (1963). *Improvisation for the theater. A handbook of teaching and directing techniques* (1st ed.). Northwestern University Press.

Sprenger, M. (2020). *Social emotional learning and the brain: Strategies to help your students thrive.* ASCD.

Snyder, S. C. & Fenner, D. S. (2021). *Culturally responsive teaching for multilingual learners: Tools for equity.* Corwin Press.

The National Office of Disease Prevention and Health Promotion. (2022) *Healthy people 2030.* https://health.gov/healthypeople/objectives-and-data/browse-objectives/physical-activity

The U.S. Department of Health and Human Services. (2018). *Physical activity guidelines for Americans.* https://www.cdc.gov/healthyschools/physicalactivity/guidelines

Vaughn, K., & Winner, E. (2000). SAT scores of students who study the arts: What we can and cannot conclude about the association. *Journal of Aesthetic Education, 34*(3/4), 77–89.

Wagner, T. (2012). *Creating innovators: The making of young people who will change the world.* Scribner.

Willis, J., & Willis, M. (2020). *Research-based strategies to ignite student learning: Insights from neuroscience and the classroom* (revised and expanded ed.). ASCD.

Yazzie-Mintz, E. (2010). *Charting the path from engagement to achievement: A report on the 2009 high school survey of student engagement.* Center for Evaluation & Education Policy.

2 Getting Ready to Move

Picture This....

I just finished an artist-in-residency at the Integrated Arts Academy (IAA), a diverse local elementary school in Vermont. The school is diverse because Burlington, VT is a resettlement city for refugees coming from a variety of countries that are experiencing conflict, war, and a slew of other hardships. In this school, there are 48 different home languages spoken, and 16% of students are currently receiving some kind of EL service. The majority of students are from the Congo, Somalia, and Vietnam, with a new group of students and families currently immigrating from Afghanistan. This makes for a rich school culture and an incredible opportunity for students to learn from other students who have a variety of life experiences and perspectives. It also presents some challenges for schools with students coming to school often after experiencing trauma, sometimes having little experience with school, and with varying levels of English language proficiency.

While working with this diverse population, I renewed my belief in the power of the arts to transform the learning environment, providing a space for all students to participate, succeed, and feel a sense of belonging. I will never forget the moment when I looked up during a lesson integrating dance with geometry, and saw 24 first-grade students all moving at the same time, fully engaged, and rehearsing their *math dance* (see Figure 2.1). This was a lesson on the similarities between what mathematicians and choreographers do: they make shapes, they count (lots and lots of counting), they solve problems, they make patterns, they use their imaginations, and they collaborate. The students began by figuring out as a group three shapes

DOI: 10.4324/9781003296317-2

Figure 2.1 First-grade students rehearse their *math dance*
(Photograph taken by author with permission from IAA)

they could make with their bodies (working as mathematicians), and then they were asked to work together to explore what ways these shapes could move through space (working as choreographers). As I played music in the background, and groups began working, I stopped for a moment to video-tape the rehearsal, and I was stunned. Every student was actively engaged, moving, talking about shapes, and working together effectively: students whose first language was not English, students who might not regularly participate, students struggling with social and emotional issues, and students with special needs.

This level of engagement by all students was not an anomaly during the two-week residency, it was the norm. Most of the classroom teachers commented on how engaged students were, especially noting the active participation of students who do not often participate. In one kindergarten class, I caught a math lesson prior to my workshop and noticed a child who walked out of the room two times during the lesson and rolled around the rug the rest of time, but when the music was on and the class was moving, this child was locked in. I know what you must be thinking: "But what you were doing was play time! I have to teach math at some point"—and yes … you do. But if you integrate movement with math, there is going to be a difference in engagement and student behaviors, which ultimately results in deeper learning.

Getting kids up and moving around the room and out of their desks can be frightening at first. Often teachers prefer to have students in their seats or at appointed spaces on the rug as it helps to maintain order. I say, let's move those chairs and desks aside to make a bigger space to move.

However, there are steps needed to get there, so that both students and teachers feel a sense of safety and order in this new environment.

This chapter prepares you and your students for doing creative work: establishing boundaries and creating a conducive environment. It includes activities to teach and practice some of the necessary skills to ensure that students have safe bodies, are ready to work in a collaborative and supportive way, and know what the logical consequences are for not engaging appropriately. Some foundational concepts are explored with suggestions for activities to practice these skills. Lesson plans for these activities are at the end of the chapter.

Routine and Novelty: Finding the Balance Between the Two

As teachers, we know that routine is paramount. Kids feel safe when they know the schedule, what to expect, and what comes next, which is central to their learning (Sprenger, 2020). It is, therefore, important to make sure to set up a similar routine when you do creative and active lessons in your classroom. Start with expectations, move into a warm-up, dive into your main lesson that often includes students working together to create a work, and end with a share and reflection. This kind of routine sends a message that creative work is work too, and students can see that the arch of the lesson is similar to other content areas covered in school.

However, creating novelty, shaking that routine up a bit, and adding an element of surprise can also have a positive impact on children and their learning. In Mariale Hardiman's (2012) *Brain Targeted Teaching Method,* she explains that one of the reasons why the arts are so effective is that it provides novelty. Novelty, Hardiman argues, wakes up the brain. When things are always the same, the amygdala (the part of the brain that is dedicated to sensing danger and is prepared for either a fight or flight reflex) basically says "ok, we are good, now relax." While we know it is essential for students to feel calm to learn (if there is any anxiety, information literally does not pass through the amygdala into long-term memory), especially for our students who may have experienced trauma, the downside is that this relaxed mode isn't always optimal for learning. Moving the desks in your classroom, signaling that something will be different in the learning environment, causes the brains of these young ones to think: "ok, wake up, something is different here. I need to pay attention." For students who need routine to feel safe, it can help to give these students fair warning for any such change in their days' activities. Taking a moment to check in with students that may thrive on routine is a great way to ensure they feel safe and ready for something new.

Ok, I Moved the Desks Aside, Now What?!

Having students up and moving and more active in the classroom may be a new and scary venture for some educators. This chapter can provide some structures that prepare both you and your students for working in a different way. As a good teacher, you know that effective classroom management is essential for learning and that children need boundaries. While the activities in this book allow for more "out of seat" time and thus more freedom in the classroom, this doesn't mean a free for all. There are clear rules of engagement that have to be maintained to keep the work effective. Establishing these expectations is key to success. However, keep in mind that this way of behaving in the classroom may be foreign to some students, and in the beginning, they may act in unexpected ways. It will take some time for them to figure out a new way to behave in this active classroom. Be patient and consistent and once students understand that there are expectations for this new way of learning, they will get on board and get down to learning.

Engagement is a key component of classroom management. Since many of these activities are fun, and look and sound different than a typical lesson, there tends to be less issues with unexpected behaviors. As students see the benefits of this kind of work (it's more active, they often work with peers, and they have more choice and autonomy), you may see less of a need for classroom management.

Two Thumbs Up for Establishing Boundaries and Agreements

Before starting any active lesson, which encourages students to take risks (i.e., getting in front of their peers and sometimes acting a little silly as well as being more physically engaged with their classmates), it is important to establish the boundaries. In effort to participate, students must agree to two things: safety (with bodies and feelings) and to try everything (at least once). Asking for two thumbs up from each student in acknowledgment of their agreement is an important way to start every lesson and make those boundaries clear.

Agreement 1: Safety First

Safety with Bodies

First, students need to agree to be safe with both the bodies and feelings of themselves and their classmates. Safety with bodies is first and foremost. When you move the chairs aside for the first time, there is a greater sense of freedom for students to move their bodies, and it may signal to them that there are no boundaries. Students may see this as an opportunity to let it loose. For example, in the **pass the sound and movement** activity (see Box 2.1), students are encouraged to share a movement with

---

Pass the Sound and Movement

This quick and fun warm up game is a great way to change the energy in your classroom and prime students to work both physically and creatively. Have students make one large circle and explain that the game acts like a wave (one person makes a wave move and it travels all around the circle). Practicing this once is helpful. Students will now pass around their own move. One student makes a move (wiggles their torso, shakes their head, or the ever-popular disco move) and passes it to the student next to them, who tries to mimic it. Remind students to use eye contact and to do their best to imitate the move (but it doesn't have to be exact). This move is passed around the circle until it comes back to the person who started it. Now the next person makes up a new move and passes it around the circle until all students have had a turn creating and passing a movement. Play uptempo music to add to the positive energy! (Note: give students a few minutes to come up with a move before playing so that the game doesn't stop, while kids think of an idea. It has to move quickly or the energy drops and it's no longer fun. As students work, push them to do the moves as fast as they can!)

Box 2.1 Pass the Sound and Movement Activity to Increase Energy in Your Classroom and Set the Tone for Fun and Active Learning

the class that will be mimicked by their classmates as it is passed around the circle. Without a doubt, if the expectation is not established before the activity that bodies are to remain standing, there is always one student who will immediately throw their body on the ground and do the worm (a breakdance move from the 80s where you move your body to look like a worm inching across the floor).

Establishing how to be safe with each other is also paramount. Since these activities push the normal boundaries of student-to-student contact, for example, students might be asked to hold hands, touch shoulders, or put legs or feet together, it is imperative that you discuss what it means to engage with each other physically in a safe way. This includes being gentle and asking before touching to make sure their classmate is comfortable doing so. For example, the activity **sculptor and clay** (see Box 2.2) requires one student to act as a sculptor and to shape their partner as if a lump of clay into a human sculpture. With this activity, students practice saying: "Can I move your arm in the air like this?" and "Is it ok to touch your shoulder?" Students interact with each other in physical ways on the playground and in gym class, so they tend to know where the line is, but it is important to remind them when you do this kind of work to ensure all

Sculptor and Clay

Place students in pairs. Ask one student to be the sculptor and one the clay. Explain what a sculptor does (or show a video clip or picture). The student who is the sculptor will move their partner's body in various ways, working to get them into a pose that looks like a sculpture. In doing so, students need to practice asking their partner: "Is it ok that I move your arm like this?" or "Is it ok to touch this part of your shoulder?" etc. Encourage students to be creative and to try a variety of poses before they settle on their final piece. After a designated time, ask students to stop. Have all the artists walk around the room and do a gallery walk to see all the varied works. Artists may speak about their work. Then switch roles with the clay now becoming the sculptor. At the end, be sure to process together, asking students how it felt to do the activity, what worked well, and what did students notice about the works created.

Box 2.2 Sculpture and Clay Activity to Teach Safety with Bodies

students feel safe and to be thoughtful and careful with how they engage with each other physically.

Activities to Practice Safety

In effort to accomplish a safe learning environment, students need to practice moving in an open space as well as navigating this space with their classmates. Try these two activities to prepare your students for an active classroom. Lesson plans for these activities are shared at the end of the chapter, but the implementation for them is explored more fully here to help guide you in this important process of setting expectations for creative work.

Freeze is an excellent introductory activity to lead with a new group of students. It accomplishes two important things in your classroom. First, it provides the students an opportunity to practice moving safely around the room. Second, it gives you a tool to stop the action if anything seems unsafe. The game starts like *Simon Says,* with the teacher calling out actions for students to do (jump, wiggle, walk on tiptoes, etc.). You call "freeze" in between commands and ask that students freeze their entire bodies (even their mouths), focus eyes on you, and get ears ready for the next direction. *Freeze* can start with simple actions and then quickly involve more drama: "walk as if in peanut butter" or "splash in the puddles." The key aspect of this activity for establishing expectations is the way you offer feedback. Comments such as, "Wow, look at this student, even their eyes are frozen" or "Wow, even mouths are frozen" and "Thank you for all your eyes," reinforces what you expect. Since students have practiced the skill, "freeze" becomes a cue in your classroom to immediately stop the action and give their attention to you. And you will have to use it. When kids get excited about their scene work, there are times when they get some funny ideas and think it's ok to do x, y, or z (maybe use the desk as a jumping off point for their scene about diving into the ocean). In these instances, you can call "freeze" and are able to stop the action before it starts. Not only can you play this game to set expectations, but it is great to use as a warm up for the day to get kids up and moving and ready to learn. It should be revisited often to reinforce safety expectations.

Bubbles acts in a similar way to *freeze,* in that it provides you with both practice and language to support student safety in the classroom.

This activity, however, is often a better starting point for younger students in kindergarten and first grade. Students are encouraged to blow up their own invisible bubble that creates their own personal space and practice moving around the space with their classmates while keeping a safe distance. See the **bubbles** lesson plan at the end of the chapter for more directions on how to lead this activity in your classroom.

Safety with Feelings

In addition to being safe with bodies, students need to be safe with each other's feelings. This ensures that the group works to be supportive, laughs with classmates not at anyone, and is always inclusive. Since many of the activities in this book require performing in front of their peers, it is important that you clearly establish the expectations for both performing and observing. Sometimes students view observing as a time to check out, so it can be helpful to explain what an important role observing has in the performing arts. The main artforms introduced in this book are theater and dance, which are intended to be performed for an audience. Explain to students that the audience helps to shape a work of art. A new play, for example, often has a preview week where audiences are invited to see a show in its early stages and writers and directors can see how their work is being received and make any necessary changes needed to increase impact or clarity. Also explain how a work of art is often interpreted in relation to the viewer. While an artist often has an idea or feeling they are trying to communicate with a work of art, the viewer responds to the artwork, bringing their own lens and set of experiences, which often results in either a different or new perspective.

Establishing the role of the observer is important to ensure that the process of sharing work is both a safe and productive part of the learning process. It is good to discuss how it can feel scary to be up in front of their classmates. Therefore, being an attentive observer is important for making their classmates feel safe. If a person whispers or giggles to a neighbor when students are performing, they might assume they are whispering something unkind. Better not to talk while their classmates are performing. (See Box 2.3: *1,2,3 action* for how to establish quiet and attentiveness when performances start.) It is also important to discuss the difference between laughing with and laughing at (which can be done with some role play and acting out of scenarios).

Figure 2.2

1,2,3 Action is a structure to help support effective performing and observing as it signals when the performance will start and, thus, the observers must listen. It mimics the black and white movie clapper used by movie directors to cue the action. Students are asked to raise their arms in the air making a huge "clapper" and count "1,2,3, action" together. On "action," students clap their arms together. This is a helpful structure so you don't have to spend a lot of time trying to keep students quiet during the performance process. It allows for a bit of last-minute rehearsal. While this is occurring, students can chat quietly. But when students say they are ready to perform, it's time to cue the role of the observer (voices off, eyes on the speakers, body in the direction of the performers) and let the *action* begin!

Box 2.3 Activity 1,2,3 Action

Activity to Practice Being an Observer

My Journey Today (see full lesson plan at the end of this chapter) is one of the best ways to establish the importance of both the performer and especially the observer. In this activity, students spend a few minutes (in their own bubble) "acting out" their day from beginning to the present moment. Once students have had some rehearsal time, ask half of the class to perform their day. The other half of the class is asked to be observers and offer feedback with sentence starters: "I notice" and "I wonder." The activity builds the capacity of students to be active observers and to be attentive as students perform. It also builds connections between students as they respond to each other's performances and in some cases find out new things they have in common.

Agreement 2: Try Everything ... (at Least Once)

The second agreement is to give everything a try. When introducing this expectation to students, you can call it the "broccoli effect" because trying a new activity is like trying broccoli. You might not want to try it because you aren't sure if you are going to like it. However, it's good for you (both broccoli and the creative process!). In the same way, ask students to at least try an activity first before saying if they like it or not. Just like trying broccoli, students might need to try activities a few times before they like it.

After reviewing the two rules for engagement: safety and trying everything, it is helpful to ask students to give you a two thumbs up signal before you start any lesson. *Most* of the time, all students will show their agreement with two thumbs up. There are always a few students that may resist at first or try to test the boundaries by hiding their thumbs. If this happens, first just address the child directly by asking if they can abide by the agreements. Often by addressing them directly they will agree. If they do not, ask them to sit out for a minute and observe, then work hard to encourage them to join in eventually. Kids usually want to be with the group, so in most cases, they eventually will agree to follow the expectations. When the activities begin and students see how much fun they are going to have, there tends to be no issues with agreements. Once you have this language established, you can and should use it. If you see something that seems unsafe ask students: "Are you being safe with your friends' feelings? Do you remember our agreements?" If students break these rules after a reminder, it is time for them to take a break or "take 5" (a more creative term for "take a break").

Take 5

The goal of any lesson is to have all involved and actively engaged, but there are times when students break their agreements after being given ample reminders. In this case, you can ask students to "take 5," a phrase that is used on a movie set. During a film shooting, a director might call out "take 5" which signals the actors to take a few minutes break to regroup, or it can be used for both actors and directors to think about how to best move forward. Using this terminology instead of the more prevalent classroom structure of "take a break" keeps things in the creative world, but is similar enough that the signal is clear to students- it's time to take a few minutes to get refocused.

When introducing "take 5," explain how it is used on a movie set and how it will be used in your classroom. If the teacher calls "take 5" that means the student needs to find a space in the room, a bit off to the side, to refocus. It is helpful to have students take a 5-minute break or take five cleansing breaths, and to think about what they need to do to come back and be ready to work more effectively. It works well to have students put a thumb up on their knee to signal that they feel ready to return, but that you establish that you will call them back in when you feel they are ready to return. (A timer can be helpful in this process.) The goal of "take 5" is to make this a constructive process, not a punitive one. If you think about a movie set, there are times when even adults need to take a minute: either they have become frustrated, a bit tired, or even argumentative over a creative decision. Often taking a break helps all move forward in a more productive way.

Community-Building & Collaboration

The Importance of Building Community

In addition to establishing agreements and boundaries, it is essential to build a supportive community in your classroom. While building community is key to any learning environment, it is even more vital in a creative space as a bit more risk is involved when students are asked to perform in front of their peers. Explain the importance of working together to create an environment where students feel like they can try something new and get the support of their peers. In doing so, it is essential to make sure that all feel included. One specific way this comes up is when groups are made. There are times when the activities call for students to make their own groups, and when doing so, it is important to ensure that all students can join any group no matter what. It can be helpful to "act out" how this looks by showing them, for example, what it looks like when someone feels welcome to join a group, and when it does not look that way, and how body language can be used both in a positive or negative way to this end. The key to ensuring that a strong community is maintained is by continuing to reinforce all the agreements and expectations that have been established with positive language such as: "Thanks for making your classmates feel included, that helps us build a creative community" and "Thanks for being great observers, this helps our performers feel safe to share their work" as well as reminding language "I noticed that folks were talking during that share, let's remember our agreement to be supportive observers" or "I noticed some bodies were a bit out of control, let's refocus and make sure we are being safe."

The second part of this chapter presents some activities to build a strong and supportive community for arts integrated lessons. These activities help to establish trust between students, allowing them to begin to learn how to collaborate effectively and practice turning on their imaginations for creative learning.

Learning How to Collaborate: Foundational Skills

One of the strongest skills gained from working in the creative realm is learning how to collaborate. Our students will be joining a workforce where teams are central to how work is done, and yet the skills needed to work effectively in teams is rarely explicitly taught in schools. Moreover, collaboration is hard to do. There are so many factors that go into collaboration: speaking up and listening (and knowing when to do each), leadership and following (and knowing when to do each). Collaboration takes effective communication which is also not always explicitly taught in schools. In effort to create a space where working together is not only the norm, but done effectively, it's important to teach the skills necessary to be effective communicators and to give students opportunities to build these skills through practice (Knight, 2015).

Leadership/Following

An ideal vision of collaboration in a classroom would be students in groups taking turns, listening, and giving and taking ideas. Unfortunately, too often there is one student who immediately takes charge and a few that try to hide in the periphery. However, to be most effective in a group setting, all participants need to be both leaders and followers. If one person constantly leads activities, there is going to be only one way to solve problems, one perspective, and a limited range of possibilities. It is important that you find ways to encourage shared leadership in your classroom. Your role as a facilitator can help accomplish this goal. As students are working, circulate and give friendly reminders that all participants should have a chance to share ideas. You can also assign jobs, for example, assign a director for each group when they are working on a task. Teach what a good director does, which is to listen to the actors, take all ideas in, but if need be make the final decision for next steps. Reflecting after group activities can also help your students learn how to effectively collaborate. Ask questions such as: "What helped your group accomplish this task?" or "How did your group work together effectively? What were the challenges and successes?" As you do more collaborative work in your classroom, which is often if you are using activities from this book, you will see students improve in the skills necessary to do this work. When groups share work, it is always clear which groups work effectively together as their work is always exemplary. Using this as a discussion point for the group helps to instill how working as a group, sharing leadership and giving and taking of ideas, always results in a stronger end result. Like any skill, practice is the best way to improve, so doing this kind of work in your classroom offers your students a chance to practice and build collaboration skills.

Activity to Practice Shared Leadership

Diamonds (end of this chapter)

Active Listening

When you think of group work, you might think of someone taking charge, giving directions, and making decisions. In reality, listening is one of the most important skills for effective communication which is essential to collaboration (Knight, 2015). A group of students needs to be able to be fully present, work to hear what their classmates are trying to express and explain, and put that into action. This is what is meant by active listening. It is listening for understanding and responding to the communication in some way. Listening is so important for learning in the classroom, and yet it is a skill that is not explicitly taught in schools. One of the best ways to teach listening skills is through improvisation (see Chapter 3). Theater improvisation, the art of making up dialogue on the spot after being given scenarios to act out, requires a high level of listening. Participants must be fully present and not thinking about anything else. They need to not only hear what their partner says, but be able to process it quickly and react.

Lessons to Practice Listening

> *Freeze improvisation game* (Chapter 3)
> *Brown bag improv* (Chapter 3)

Interdependence

Due to the collaborative nature of theater and dance, it is a great way to teach and reinforce the idea that we are more successful when we work together. As discussed above, this is an idea that is a natural result of creative collaborative work in the classroom. As students work in groups to accomplish tasks (making up scenes, developing a dance, creating sculptures), they begin to experience how as a group they can accomplish amazing things. Each activity in this book requires students to practice these skills. To introduce the idea of interdependence, try the *Rock Passing Game from Ghana*.

Lesson for Teaching Interdependence

> *Rock passing game from Ghana* (end of this chapter)

LESSON PLANS

 ## Bubbles

Grades K-2

Bubbles is a fun way to teach personal body space and instill a safe working environment for your classroom. Children blow up imaginary bubbles around their bodies and move around the room to music. Their goal is to *not* pop any of their classmates' bubbles or their own. This is a foundational lesson that will allow students to practice being safe with their bodies and prepare them for the movement activities in this book.

What You Need

- An open space
- Slow flowing music (classical or new age)

Student Learning Objective

Students will move safely in a variety of spatial relationships and formations with other dancers, sharing, and maintaining personal space.

How to Do the Activity

1. When the space in your classroom is cleared, ask students what is different about the space? Have them name what is missing.
2. Explain that this new space is different from their typical classroom to provide plenty of room to move around. Tell students that while engaging in this type of work, they will move a lot, including big and bold movements such as rolling, jumping, leaping, and "running" (a slower run than is done on a playground). Therefore, they must be extra careful with their bodies and the bodies of their classmates.
3. Ask each of the students to blow a large imaginary bubble around their bodies, making sure their entire body is covered from nose to toes.
4. Explain that the object of the game is to move around the space without popping each other's bubbles or having their own bubble pop.
5. If their bubble pops, they should quickly apologize (saying "sorry, I popped your bubble"), blow another bubble, and resume play.

6. Play slow music and let the students move around the space.
7. If your students need a challenge, create a smaller space using chairs or tape or play faster music.

Helpful Hint

Kids are kids and there are always going to be a few who push the boundaries and try to pop each other's bubbles. The best way to handle it is to first stop and remind them of the goal. Next, stop and ask how many bubbles were popped and challenge them to try again popping less. If a student is still popping bubbles, it might be time for them to **take 5**!

Reflect and Wrap Up

Ask your students:

* How many students were able to make it through the whole activity without their bubble popping?
* What did you need to do to keep your bubble and your friend's bubbles safe? Students will hopefully suggest they had to look carefully (keeping their eyes open), be attentive at all times, and be aware of their personal space not getting too close to their neighbors.

Extensions or Adaptations

Try "**freeze**" which is the next level of this activity.

Standards Addressed

NCAS. DA: Pr5.1.2. b. Move safely in a variety of spatial relationships and formations with other dancers, sharing and maintaining personal space.

Freeze

Grades K-6

Freeze, like bubbles, helps students practice safety in this new open space, preparing the way for incorporating more movement into your lessons. This activity can replace *bubbles* for older students or be an extension of *bubbles*. In this fun game, students practice stopping when you call out "freeze!" A freeze is defined as a frozen body: no talking, eyes on the teacher, and ready for the next direction. By giving fun directions like skip, wiggle, slow motion, and leap, students get to expend some energy, practice gross motor skills, and learn a necessary skill for creative work (safety and body awareness). This game should be repeated often as a reminder or used as a warm-up for future lessons.

What You Need

- An open space
- Music

Student Learning Objective

Students will move safely in a variety of spatial relationships and formations with other dancers, sharing and maintaining personal space.

How to Play the Game

1. After moving the desks aside, ask students what is different about the space. Explain that when they are engaging in movement activities in the classroom, they will be participating in activities that will allow and require them to make big and bold movements with their bodies. They will be able to roll, jump, and leap. This will require some extra care and attention in effort to keep everyone safe. Explain that you will call "freeze" when you see any action that looks unsafe and also to signal the need to stop and listen to directions.
2. In effort to practice, ask the students to find an open space in the room. Tell them that when they hear "freeze" they must freeze like a frozen icicle (no moving, eyes on speaker, ears ready to listen.) Give a direction like: "walk around the room." Walking is a great way to start the game. Students may walk in any way they choose. (Playing music during this activity can be helpful and fun.)
3. After a minute, call out "freeze." Make sure you have everyone's eyes before you give the next direction. If you don't you can say: "I need all eyes" or you can thank students for giving you your eyes.
4. When all bodies are frozen, give the next direction, such as "hop on one foot."
5. Other directions may include: skip, march, roll, wiggle, crab walk, side step, dance, leap, run in slow motion, and run at medium speed.

6. If the students have done the activity bubbles, be sure to refer back to that concept. Ask if students are keeping their bubbles intact.

Extension and/or Adaptation

This format can be used with any unit to set the mood or create an experiential learning opportunity. For example, if you have a unit on seasons, you can have children walk as if through a foot of snow in winter, skip and splash in the puddles during spring, crunch through the leaves in fall, or walk on hot concrete during summer. Another idea is to practice "emotions" such as walking as if late for school, walking as if going to take a really hard test, waking as if you are tired, and walking as if you just won a $100. The adaptations are endless.

Standards Addressed

NCAS. DA: Pr5.1.2. b. Move safely in a variety of spatial relationships and formations with other dancers, sharing and maintaining personal space.

Diamonds

Grades K-6

This activity has students working in groups to both create movements and mimic their classmates' movements. They must work together to all move as one which requires focus and awareness. This is a great activity for calming and focusing students. It also helps practice collaboration, shared leadership, and group awareness.

What You Need

- Open space
- Slow and calming music
- Picture of a diamond

Student Learning Objective

Students will collaborate with diverse partners to engage in a movement activity where they explore and experiment with a variety of locomotor movements, both creating and repeating movements of their classmates and demonstrating awareness of self and others in space.

43

How to Do the Activity

1. Show a picture of a diamond shape explaining that there are four points.
2. Explain that students will work in groups of four to make a diamond on the floor, while standing (see Figure 2.3).
3. The student who is at the point of the diamond moves their arms to the music in a slow manner. As they do, the other three mimic these moves working to move at the same time so that it is hard to know who the leader is.
4. When the leader has finished, they turn to the right. Since all the other players follow the leader, they all turn to the right, and there is a new leader.
5. Complete the entire cycle so that each student has a chance to lead. It is helpful to repeat this at least twice. Ask students to continue until all teams have completed the task.
6. Once all students have practiced this a few times, ask half of the class to perform, and the other class to observe.
7. Discuss and reflect.

Figure 2.3 Students play *Diamonds*, an activity to teach group awareness

Helpful Hint

Encourage students to move slowly so they can move as one. They often want to move quickly or do a silly dance, but remind them to keep it simple and to just move their arms and hands. When they are given this constraint, it pushes them to get creative and more fully explore all the ways they can move their arms. Coach leaders by reminding them to move at a pace that their team can stay with them. Slow music is very helpful for this process.

Reflect and Wrap Up

- Ask performers how it felt to perform in front of their peers. Since this is an introductory activity, you are working to build their confidence. Also ask, what was needed to make the activity work? (Hopefully, they respond with: moving slowly, thinking about your partners, focus, etc.)
- Ask observers what they noticed about the performances. When teams function effectively and are focused, they can create something amazing to watch. This will hopefully spark a conversation about what a group can accomplish when they work as a team.

Adaptations/Extensions

For younger students: This activity works for all age groups. With students in K-2, you might skip the performance/reflection aspect of the lesson. You may also want to try it in a whole group with you leading (and then asking for a few volunteers to lead).

For integrating with content: This framework can be used with any content. It is especially useful for science (water cycle, plant cycle, or life cycles). It can also be used in social studies (see lesson plan *Diamonds & The Civil Rights Movement* in Chapter 5).

Standards Addressed

NCAS. DA:Cr1.1.1. b. Explore a variety of locomotor and non-locomotor movements by experimenting with and changing the elements of dance.

NCAS. DA:Pr5.1.2. c. Repeat movements, with an awareness of self and others in space. Self-adjust and modify movements or placements.

My Journey Today

Grades K-6

Students use gestures and movement to demonstrate what they have done in their day. As students work individually and then in groups, they can both experience the power of both performance and observation. This exercise can be used for many outcomes, but it is especially impactful for exemplifying the importance of the role of the observer as they are tasked with identifying what they notice and wonder about their classmates' movements.

What You Need

- Open space
- Music

Student Learning Objective

Students will identify artistic choices made in a drama work through participation and observation.

How to Do the Activity

1. Ask students to find a space in the room where they can have their own "bubble" or area to work. Ask them to think about their day so far. How did it start? What things did they do throughout the day leading up to this class?
2. Ask them to use their bodies to "act out" their days so far. (Tell students that they should not be looking at each other's work, but just focusing on their movements. They can even turn away from their classmates.)
3. Put on music and give students a few minutes to rehearse.
4. Next, ask half of the students to perform their "day's journey." (This is only mimed, no talking). Ask students to stand still with their hands at their sides when they are done. When all the students have finished, stop the music.
5. Ask the observers to share one thing they noticed and wondered about the performer's actions. (Eg. "I noticed that Student A was moving their arms up and down at the beginning, I wonder if they were brushing their teeth?" Or "I wonder if X lives really far from school, it seems like they were walking for a long time.")

6. After a handful of students have shared observations, allow the performer to respond to the comments made, then switch groups.

Reflect and Wrap Up

This activity is all about the reflection! The idea is to reinforce how theater is all about communication. By engaging the observer fully in this exercise, asking them what they noticed/wondered about, and making inferences about what their classmates did during their day, they can experience what it takes to communicate effectively through gesture and movement. It is immediate feedback that is given by classmates and not you!

Some driving questions:

• How did it feel to perform for your classmates?
• How did it feel when your classmates noticed something you did on stage?
• What did you notice about the way your classmates used their bodies to tell stories? What were some strategies that worked well?
• What might you do to make your actions more clear to your audience?

Extensions/Adaptations

For younger students: You may just want to focus on the performing aspect. Ask all students to mime their day all at the same time, while you act as the observer. You can comment on what you noticed and wondered. Use this to reinforce key ideas about using the bodies to tell stories, such as "I can tell you walked to school, I can see that you used a marching motion. Was I correct? Wow, you really used your body to show me about your day." Note: This is a fantastic way for you as a teacher to (a) get to know more about your students and (b) see how their morning routine went, which can help you meet their needs more fully.

Literacy. Have students act out the journey of a character from a chapter book or read aloud.

Social Studies. Have students act out the day in the life of a person in a certain time period (day on the Oregon Trail or day of a child living in colonial times.)

47

Science. Have students act out the journey of a monarch butterfly or other migrating animal.

Standards Addressed

NCAS. TH:Re7.1.4.a. Identify artistic choices made in a drama/theatre work through participation and observation.

Rock Passing Game from Ghana

Grades 1–6

In this game, students learn about interdependence. In effort to move the rocks around the circle, all students must work together effectively. Even one student off rhythm or unfocused will stop the game. Each student has a rock that they pass while singing a song and doing a rhythm pattern. The goal is to all work as a team to move the rocks around the circle.

What You Need

- Open space, circle rug for sitting
- Music: Preferably recording or Rock Passing Game (available on YouTube).
- Maps: Ghana and Africa
- Rocks: One for each student

Student Learning Objective

Students will work together to accomplish a task, assuming shared responsibility for collaborative work.

How to Do the Activity

1. Show a map of Ghana and Africa (see Box 2.4 about the need for cultural responsiveness). Discuss how kids anywhere in the world make up games with what they have. What kinds of games do kids play in the United States that need nothing but what they have available to them (hide and go seek, tag, clapping games).
2. Teach the tune and lyrics (see lyrics below).
3. Teach them the rhythm which is on the count of 4. Have students clap a four-count rhythm.

Cultural Responsiveness. It is important when engaging in activities, songs, and dances from other cultures, that you provide the context and learning needed to ensure you are being culturally responsive. Students should learn where these traditions come from and that they should be done with acknowledgment and understanding of the culture they were created in. Before playing *Rock Passing Game from Ghana*, be sure to provide some learning about Ghana. Show a map of Ghana and of Africa, so students can see where the game originated.

Box 2.4 Attending to Cultural Responsiveness while Playing *Rock Passing Game*

4. Teach the actions first by chanting the actions together without having children use rocks. (Pick up. Tap. Tap. Pass. Pick up. Tap. Tap. Pass)
5. Now practice the actions without rocks. Explain that they will use their right hand. They will pick up the rock that the person next to them has dropped close to them. Then they tap the rock twice in front of them and then pass to their right side. This takes all four counts of the music. Practice this a few times saying the chant. Then practice with the song.
6. Give each student a rock. Try the game with rocks, song, and passing.

Song:
Obwisana sa nana
Obwisana sa
Obwisana sa nana
Obwisana sa.

(Translation)
The rock has crushed my hand, grandma
The rock has crushed my hand
The rock has crushed my hand, grandma
The rock has crushed my hand

Helpful Hints

The more you direct this, the better it will go. When you first give students rocks, it is best to practice without passing until all students are in rhythm and seem to be moving in tandem. Coach in rhythm (saying you will let them know when to actually MOVE the rock), chanting: "Pick up. Tap. Tap. Pass. Pick up. Tap. Tap. Pass. next time pass the rock, ready go. Pick up. Tap. Tap. Pass." Then ask them to start singing, while you keep chanting the directions. The first couple of times, you might have one student who can't get it. And they will end up with a pile of rocks in front of them. All good. Just stop, redistribute rocks so all have one, and try again. The challenge is to make it work and learn how all have to work together to do so.

Extensions/Adaptations

For younger students, simplify the pattern; have them do a three-count pattern: pick up-tap-pass. (They will naturally pick up the rock and do a rest beat if you lead it.)

Social Studies connection: Learn more about Ghana and about games and songs children play there and make more connections to games/songs that children play in the US.

Science connection: Use this as a morning meeting game when studying rocks. Have students collect and identify rocks prior to playing the game.

Standards Addressed

21st C. skill: Collaborate with others: Assume shared responsibility for collaborative work, and value the individual contributions made by each team member.

C3. D2.Geo.6.K-2. Identify some cultural and environmental characteristics of specific places.

References

Hardiman, M. (2012). *Brain targeted teaching model for 21st-century schools*. Corwin.

Knight, J. (2015). *Better conversations: Coaching ourselves and each other to be more credible, caring, and connected*. Corwin.

Sprenger, M. (2020). *Social emotional learning and the brain: Strategies to help your students thrive*. ASCD.

3 | Setting the Stage for Success

Picture This....

I decided to write this book for many reasons, but especially because there didn't seem to be enough resources for me when I started to do this work as a young teacher. I too often would see social studies textbooks, for example, with a suggestion for dramatic exploration that would say things like "act out the Battle of the Bulge." First of all, can you imagine doing this with a classroom of 25 5th graders? And secondly, it gave no structures to do so. You can't just dramatize a historical event from scratch with students who have no experience acting or improvising. Perhaps you could find a script or play written about a historical event to act out in class or a script of a fable to integrate theater with literacy. However, I believe it is the process of your students creating the dramatic scenes themselves that greatly impacts their learning. This chapter aims to help you build a foundation for doing theater and movement work in your classroom, so when you get to the social studies chapter that says "consider dramatizing the Battle of the Bulge" or a literacy lesson that says "act out the plot of this story," you will be ready with structures and skills in place to do so effectively. Many of the concepts included in this chapter are built off the work of many theater artists and educators especially Viola Spolin's foundational work *Improvisation for the theater* (1963).

DOI: 10.4324/9781003296317-3

Theater Basics

There are a few key concepts to teach and reinforce in your classroom to help your students be successful at many of the activities in this book, prepare them to be ready and willing to try new things, and help to create a culture that supports creativity, collaboration, and risk-taking.

Building an Ensemble

A basic premise of dance and theater work is the importance of the ensemble. The idea of the ensemble is that the group is as important or often more important than the individual. A play needs many people to participate to tell a story. In many drama schools, they spend most of their time creating an ensemble with their actors before introducing individual roles. To create an ensemble, students need to learn to listen to each other, be responsive, and work as a team. As they work in this way, students start to see that they can do more when they work with their peers. They start to build some trust and depend on each other to accomplish the creative tasks asked of them. You can use the following activities to practice building an ensemble because they require the group to work together to accomplish a task. Additionally, the importance of the ensemble and working together needs to be reinforced often in your classroom to support the creative process. Reinforcing language like: "excellent job working as a team," or "be aware of the group so you can work together to accomplish this task."

Activities for Building an Ensemble

> *Sculptures* (end of this chapter)
> *Establishing a Where* (end of this chapter)
> *Rock Passing Game from Ghana* (Chapter 2)
> *Choral Reading* (Chapter 4)

 # Key Ideas to Instill to Support Creative Work in Your Classroom

In addition to building an ensemble in your classroom, you will need to coach students to be their most creative, bold, and brave selves. The performing arts require folks to step out of their comfort zone, to push themselves to take risks, and try new things, which can be challenging for some students. There are a few key concepts that you should introduce in your active classrooms and reinforce often with your side coaching and feedback that will be explored more fully in the following section.

Be Bold, Be Brave, and Make Strong Choices

One of the most important ideas you can instill in your classroom is that students need to go for it when it comes to being dramatic. A key thing that theater can teach our students is how to take risks. Standing up in front of the class, and acting a bit silly, can be an incredibly scary thing for a young person to do, but doing so has many benefits. When students succeed and present work that is moving, funny, thoughtful, and entertaining, their peers respond favorably. This can really build students' confidence. But in order for students to take risks, there has to be a feeling of safety in the classroom. Students need to be assured if they miss the mark or act silly, that their peers will not criticize them, talk about them behind their back, laugh at not with them, or respond negatively in any way. It is vital that the teacher establishes a safe space for students to work by reinforcing the importance of safety (revisit "safety with bodies and feelings" in Chapter 2). It's also important to start small, with activities that require less risk, like all moving at the same time, before asking students to perform by themselves front and center.

As students gain some confidence, encourage them to make bold choices (see Figure 3.1, student boldly showing his move in the center of the circle). This means that instead of just doing the obvious choice, they go for it. Instead of just choosing to do a 2 on a scale of 1–10, they go for 11. What does this look like? An activity introduced by the Folger Shakespeare Library has students act out death scenes; not *Romeo and Juliet* kind of death scenes, but a comic one like is performed by Pyramus and Thisbe from *A Midsummer Night's Dream*. The script for this activity had one line: "Thus I, now die, die, die." Students were encouraged to go all out. For example, not just put their hand up to their head and sink to the ground (which is ok too), but to flail on the ground, with their body writhing, maybe even a roll, (all the while being safe and in their space, mind you). But the idea is, we want to encourage kids to make bold choices in their acting. If they are creating a scene about going shopping. Instead of just walking

Figure 3.1 Students play a leader and follower game. One student jumps to the middle to show his bold and brave move!

(Permission for photograph granted from IAA)

to the mall, maybe they crawl to the mall and they show their exhaustion because it's taken them 3 hours in the hot sun and they will not give up, they need those Air Jordans today! Reinforce this idea often in your classroom saying things like: "Is that the strongest choice you can make?" and "That was a strong choice."

It's More Than Ok to Be Silly

One of the reasons for doing drama work in the classroom is that it is just plain fun. So many of the activities in this book induce laughter for all! It is important to create a culture in your classroom where students can be a bit silly. This doesn't mean that you aren't doing good and serious work! It just means that students can let loose a little bit. Silliness goes a long way toward supporting creative work. As students feel more comfortable to take risks and be a little silly, their imaginations and creativity will thrive.

Speak Up—Please Speak Up!

If I had a dollar for every time a parent said to me at the end of one of my theater productions; "The show was great, but I wish you could teach them how to speak up!" Teaching children how to speak up is one of the most challenging parts of teaching theater, but it is such an important skill for your students (in their drama work and in the classroom). Students will need this skill to be successful in school, work, and life too. Try using the 1–10 physical scale activity (see Box 3.1) for teaching the idea of voice levels. Speaking up also has to be reinforced in your theatrical work in the classroom. Try using the idea of "able to be heard," instead of speaking louder. This focuses more on impact. Reinforce it with questions such as "Are you speaking so that you are able to be heard across the room?" Ask students to pretend as if their great grandmother who is very hard of hearing is at the back of the room, and they need to make sure she hears every word. You can also encourage students to help coach this skill with their peers. The goal of theater is to share stories with audiences. If the other students can't hear their classmates, they didn't get the job done. Instead of constantly saying: "Can you speak up so your classmates can hear you?" Try asking the audience to be the judge: "Audience, did you get all that?" and if they say no, the actors are charged to turn it up a notch.

Whole Body Scale

Ask students to stand in a circle. Tell them they are going to use their bodies to show voice levels. For example, a zero is crouched way down on the floor and a 10 is standing up tall with arms outstretched wide. As you call out each number from 0 to 10, have students vary both their voice levels and bodies to match. Start with zero which is spoken very quietly with a small body (crouched to the ground). Gradually lead students to increase their voice level and move their body higher as they move toward a big body and voice to arrive at 10. After you have this established, you can use this scale as a teaching tool. For example, ask students what body/voice level should be used for theater work? It should be a 7, which coincides with a strong theater pose (standing tall with arms at their side.). Now that kids know the scale, you can use it to reinforce expectations, such as "let's have a 3 level now" or "we need a 7 level to hear you across the stage."

Box 3.1 1–10 Whole Body Voice Scale to teach voice levels in your classroom.

The Body Is Your Instrument: Use It!

One idea that takes some time to reinforce is that when acting and dancing, the performer needs to use the whole body to communicate. This is not an idea that is supported in most school settings. Often, students are encouraged to have still bodies, which results in them being basically talking heads. Helping students learn that the body is a tool for communication is central to teaching them the art of performing. Many of the activities in this book will help your students practice this skill (see Figure 3.2), but it can be helpful to play games like charades or acting out scenarios without speaking (see scenario suggestions later in the chapter), so students learn how necessary it is to engage the body in the storytelling if they want their audience to understand what they are trying to communicate.

Lessons for Teaching Body as a Communicator

What are you doing? (end of this chapter)
Establishing a where (end of this chapter)
My journey today (Chapter 2)

Figure 3.2 Students engage in a movement activity that encourages them to use their body to convey an idea

(Photo taken with permission from IAA)

Improvisation 101

Perhaps the most useful tool in your teacher toolbox needed to integrate theater and movement into your classroom is improvisation. Improvisation or improv, as far as theater goes, is to make up dialogue on the spot to create a dramatic scene. You don't have a script, but you do have a plan. Doing improv can be tricky, but there are a few basic skills you can teach that will help you implement it into your classroom. There are also many resources available for doing this more in depth (Cahnamann-Taylor & McGovern, 2021; Spolin, 1963, 1986). There are many videos of Spolin's improv games online, which can be very helpful for seeing how they work. The basic tenets of improv will be shared here to get you started.

Say Yes

The foundational concept for improv is "Say yes!" This means that whatever is said by your partner, no matter what they decide to play in the scene, you go with it. If your partner says that they have landed on the moon, you are on the moon. If your partner says "Open your mouth wide so I can see those teeth" demonstrating that they have become a dentist, you act as if you are in the dentist chair. If you say "no" to what your partner establishes as a reality, the scene ends or just doesn't work. For example, if your partner says, "It's great being here in Italy," and you say "We aren't in Italy, we are in France," the scene is thrown off kilter and it just can't go anywhere. It becomes a tug of war and you know how that ends?! Someone is falling in the mud. Instead, teach students to "Say yes" (and act accordingly) in their improv work. They need to be attentive to their partner, listen intently, think on their feet, and be willing to be flexible and go with the flow. Sound like some important skills for your students to learn? This is why learning improvisation is such a useful tool in the classroom.

Decide on Who, What, Where in Your Scene

Because you don't have a script when you do improv, partners need to set up the scenario by making some decisions about the scene they are going to play. This requires participants to decide on *who* they are (what people do they want to be in this scene), *where* they are (where does this scene take place), and *what* is going on (often this is described as the problem to solve). Each will be described more fully in the next section. Note that when teaching improv, it is easier to start with pairs before having students work in groups. This allows the students to really practice listening and responding in a more direct way.

Establishing the Where

"Establishing the where" means choosing where a scene will take place, which can be established prior to the scene or in the midst of the scene. For example, students might decide that their scene will take place in a forest, so they begin their scene by looking up at the trees and talking about their beauty. Or in the middle of the scene, a student might open a hidden door and say: "Oh my, where are we? There are so many trees" and the scene is instantly transported to a forest. Students need to learn some skills for "establishing the where" by either what they choose to say (the improvised script) or their physicality (how they move to show they might be in a specific location). For example, they might move their hands as if they are turning a steering wheel to show they are in a car or say something like, "nothing like a nice Sunday drive to improve my mood!" Viola Spolin (1963) teaches the concept of "show not tell" which can be helpful in coaching children to use strong physicality in dramatic work. She suggests that instead of simply "telling" the audience (i.e., "Look, we are in the forest right now"), you show it (maybe you look up as if looking at tall trees, you pick up leaves off the ground, and talk about how it smells so earthy where they are.) Essentially, it is about storytelling and setting the scene versus simply giving it immediately to the audience.

Choosing the Who

When students are acting out a scenario, they need to decide on *who* the people are who are in the scene. When working in pairs, it can be helpful to be more generic (a teacher and a student, or a president and a reporter). To bring these characters to life, students use both the body as storyteller (physicalization) and the voice. Remind students to make bold choices when playing their characters. This not only makes the scenes more interesting to watch but helps the audience understand the story. Characterization is foundational to theater work, but it does present some tensions. While theater work encourages students to be bold and expressive in their portrayal of characters, there is the risk of going into stereotypes. Be sure to discuss the difference between characterization and playing stereotypes before doing any theater improvisation.

Identifying the What

The *what* in improvisation is more complex. On the most basic level, this can be what is happening in the scene (they are building a boat, climbing a mountain, traveling to a foreign country). As your student actors get more advanced in their skills, and in effort to move more fully into the world of drama, the *what* often becomes about conflict (each character wants something different in the scene) or it can be about a problem to solve (they are climbing a mountain but forget all their supplies). Creating the conflict and then showing the resolution is foundational for improvisation (and drama)!

Putting It All Together, Acting Out Scenarios

Let's see how this would work out if students were given a list of scenarios and asked to develop their own improvised scene.

Examples of Scenarios for Young People

Broke a lamp playing baseball in the house and parents are coming home soon
Didn't do their homework and they don't want to get into trouble
Found a $100 bill in the lunch room at school
Found a map to a buried treasure
Landed in a foreign land where they don't speak the language and need to get home

The students' first task would be to agree on the who, what, and where in each scene, for example, if students were given the scenario "found a map to a buried treasure," their first job would be to establish the *who*. There are a myriad of choices they could make (which is why doing this kind of work is so good for developing students' imaginations). They might choose to be two pirates or just two kids. If they decide to be two kids, the *who* can be developed even further to enhance the scene. They might decide that one of the kids is adventurous and the other is a bit of a scaredy cat, which would add to the dramatic tension. Next, they need to establish the *where*. If the students chose the pirates as the *who*, they might be on a desert island. If they chose to play kids, they could be anywhere. Maybe they are in the forest, and they notice a very old bottle under the leaves which contains a map! The *what* could simply be about figuring out what the map is describing and finding the hidden treasure. Or it could get more complex with the adventurous one ready to go to lengths to find this treasure, and the scaredy cat not wanting to go because they are afraid they will get caught by pirates! When the students rehearse their scene, it is important to remind them that they do not have to have the whole scene fully rehearsed. They need to agree upon the *who*, *what*, and *where*, and maybe try it out in a quick rehearsal. When they perform their scene for their classmates they start with a plan, but then they let it play out—they improvise! Students need to listen to their partners, respond accordingly to what is said by their partner, and let the scene go where it goes. That's improvisation.

This is just an example of how students could create an improvised scene, but it takes practice for students to get the hang of it. The basic skills of improv are foundational to many of the activities in the following chapters so they are worth practicing. Improv will be used when students act out stories, historical events, or even real-life word problems.

Lessons for Practicing Improvisation in the Classroom (all at the end of this chapter).

Establishing a Where
Freeze Improv
Brown Bag Improv

Foundational Structures for Integrating Theater and Movement into Your Classroom

Sculpture Work

Sculptures, or what has often been deemed by some as "tableaux," is a foundational skill for any theater-infused lesson. A sculpture, in this context, is a frozen picture. This frozen picture, like a sculpture you might see in a museum, has your students making a group pose that "tells" a story or embodies an idea. For example, the idea might be "freedom" or "kindness" or it might be a scene from a story like a sculpture about *Goldilocks and the Three Bears*. In these instances, all students take a pose and work together to create a frozen picture that demonstrates the idea or story (see *sculpture* lesson plan at the end of this chapter).

When introducing this skill, it's easiest to start with basic concepts that students should know well like: "summertime fun" or "sports" or an idea like "friendship" or "fear." Ask students to imagine that there is a title underneath their sculpture that describes what this sculpture is about. Students then make the sculpture that aligns with this title (see Figure 3.3). When first learning this skill, it works best to help students build these sculptures. For example, after choosing the title or theme, ask one student to make the first pose. Then, one at a time invite other students to

Figure 3.3 Students create a sculpture to respond to a read aloud
(Photo taken by author, with permission from IAA)

join the picture. You can encourage them to first see if they can relate to the person already on stage in some way before they add a new idea to the picture. This structure also helps teach students how to work as a team (especially when they are able to make sculptures on their own in groups). For example, you could name a theme for the sculpture, like "kindness," put students in groups and ask each group to find their own way to show this idea with a sculpture. Have each group share their sculpture and then discuss. This is a great way to reinforce how there are many ways to "solve" a problem, just like there are a myriad of ways to tell a story or create a work of art.

Sculptures can be used to integrate movement into a variety of lessons. In literacy class, you can have students make a sculpture for each page of a picture book, and either you can narrate in between poses or students can come up with a line to introduce their work. In social studies, students can make frozen pictures to depict historical events or a series of events. This is the basic skill that **Talking Tableaux** is built upon (see Chapter 5 for how to expand upon sculptures to create scenes.)

Sidecoaching

The idea of sidecoaching comes from Viola Spolin (1963). She suggests that as students work, you as the facilitator should give in time feedback without pausing the action. As she explains: "Sidecaoching is the calling out of just that word, that phrase, or that sentence that keeps the player [student actor] on focus. Sidecoaching phrases arise spontaneously out of what is emerging in the playing area and are given at the time players are in movement. Sidecoaching must guide players towards focus, creating interactions, movement, and transformation" (Spolin, 1986, p. 5). As you coach from the side, students get used to hearing the voice of the teacher as they work, knowing not to stop, but to take the direction and make the necessary changes. Sidecoaching is a helpful tool for teachers as it is a way to reinforce exemplary work, push students to go further with an idea, or simply change the direction of the activity. There are times where you do need to stop the action and give a clear direction. This could be for safety reasons or to re-explain the goals of the lesson if things are not working well. However, often just a bit of sidecoaching can help students move forward and improve their work. Coming up with a few phrases to use can be helpful such as "show not tell," which was introduced earlier. It is Spolin's classic phrase that encourages students to use physicalization effectively when acting and not to go for the obvious choice.

Other Helpful Sidecoaching Phrases

> *"Can you heighten the intensity?"*
> *"Can you make a more bold choice?"*
> *"Remember to work together."*
> *"Keep listening to your partner."*
> *"How can you move so that the audience knows exactly what you are trying to communicate?"*

Use of Gestures

If you take one thing away from this book, it should be the impact that using gestures has on teaching and learning. Gestures, or the use of the body, specifically the hands, to communicate, have been shown to improve learning outcomes in language acquisition (Cook et al., 2008; Glenberg, 2008; Kelly et al., 2009; Roth, 2001), increase memory and retention (Cook et al., 2008), help students understand complex concepts in math and science (Gerofsky, 2011; Glenberg, 2008; Petrick, 2012; Roth, 2001), and improve reading comprehension (Glenberg et al., 2004). The use of gestures while learning has been shown to help students better understand and remember concepts and lessen the cognitive load (Johnson-Glenberg et al., 2014; Shapiro & Stolz, 2019). The use of gestures will be covered in both the math and science chapters, but an overview is provided here so you can consider all the ways you can use the art of gesture in the teaching and learning of any subject.

One form of gesture that can be helpful for learning is iconic gesture, "a form of embodied information that 'grounds' the meaning of language in physical representations of actions and object (and perhaps even abstract concepts) that are contained in a speaker's mind" (Kelly et al., 2009, p. 314). Roth (2001) describes "iconic gesture" as a visual resemblance of what it stands for. For example, the word strong could be shown by bending arms up from the elbows to display big muscles or greater than and less than can be mimed with arms stretched out wide and hands close together.

Using gestures has been proven to be effective for both teachers and students to improve learning (Shapiro & Stolz, 2019). Shapiro and Stolz (2019) found that students learn better when teachers use gestures as the visual aspect increases understanding and it can encourage students to mimic teachers' gestures. You can create gestures with students to help them learn a poem, to review the plot in a story, or show the meaning of a concept like area or perimeter in math class. Such hand movements help students greatly in the learning process.

To integrate gestures into your teaching, you can either create them yourself and introduce them as you teach the subject or you can create them with your students. Let's say you are teaching punctuation; you could create gestures that align well with the meaning of the symbols such as a stop sign gesture to represent a period because it literally is meant to stop the sentence and a sigh (a breath and shrug of the shoulders) for a comma because it is meant to be a pause. You could also engage the students in the process by asking them all to show the meaning of a new word with a gesture and see what they come up with. Not only are they thinking and learning as they try to find the best way to show what these words mean with their bodies, but when they share them with their peers, they are repeating and practicing without feeling as if it's drill and kill. Try the lesson **Choral Reading** in Chapter 4 to see how you can create gestures with your students to learn a poem.

In addition to gestures, you can physicalize an idea, which engages more of the body. For example, if a student is explaining the cycle of a Monarch Butterfly, they can scrunch their body to act as if in a chrysalis and then spread their arms out when the butterfly breaks out of the cocoon. Glenberg (2014) argues that physically representing the action in a sentence or using gestures to understand a concept, what he calls "acting out" is key to learning. This explains how actors learn extensive amounts of lines. During the staging of a play, actors are often given blocking (or physical moves) for each line of the script they say. If they can't remember a line, doing the movement that aligns with the given line can jog their memory. This phenomenon is backed by research on acting and cognitive function (Noice & Noice, 2013).

What would "acting out" a concept look like in the classroom? It is any way of using the body to articulate an idea. In a way it is simply stringing a few gestures together to demonstrate a bigger idea. For example, if you were teaching all the parts necessary to have a complete sentence. Students might make motions to show that it starts with a capital letter (maybe they raise their arms in the air to show it's *big*), has a subject (maybe they point to themselves), verb (maybe they make a moving motion to show action), and object (maybe they point to something in the room). Then they could show that it ends with punctuation (and use their stop sign gesture). It would be really effective if students did these moves once with the terms and then again as they shared a sentence that has these same parts. Processes like metamorphosis or the water cycle are great concepts for students to "act out" and can be helpful for them in the learning process.

Lessons to Explore Using Gestures and Acting Out

> *Choral Reading* (Chapter 4)
> *Chores Warm Up* (Chapter 5)
> *Run on Sentence* (Chapter 4)

Benefits of Performance and the Role of Audience/Observer

Many of the activities in this book include an element of performance. Taking the time to have students perform for their peers is a crucial aspect of the learning process. It gives students a chance to shine and experience success at school which helps to build their confidence (Goldberg, 2021). When students see their classmates perform, they are able to see that there are many different ways to "solve the problem" (or complete the task that each of the activities requires) which helps to promote divergent thinking and creativity (Eisner, 2002). It also allows students to learn from each other. They can see the high-quality work created by their classmates, but in a way that does not emphasize comparisons. The process of performance and reflection also provides opportunities to reinforce concepts which act to deepen the learning (Hardiman, 2012). For example, if you are teaching about planets and the rotation of earth, terms, concepts, and ideas can be repeated and reinforced as you reflect and respond to the performances. After a group performs, you might ask questions such as "How did this group show how the moon rotates with the earth?" or "What type of rotation did students perform when they acted as sun and earth?" Hardiman (2012) argues that this type of reinforcement is one of the benefits of arts learning as it allows for repetition without a drill and kill method. Additionally, establishing the routine of performance and reflection supports more focused work during the rehearsal process because students know they will have to share their work at the end of class.

When students perform, encourage the other students to be active observers, emphasizing the important role that an audience has in the creative process. As Viola Spolin (1963) has taught us, there is no theater without an audience. We perform to share our stories and ideas. If the audience doesn't get what the actors are trying to communicate, then it isn't working. Ask students to be prepared to offer feedback after performances which can be used by the actors to edit and improve their work. This requires them to be fully present, pay close attention to the work being performed, and look for ways the work is effective or could change to make it stronger. Asking students to offer feedback after performances develops their abilities to be critics, helping them to learn the difference between critique and criticism. Students should also offer affirmations—sharing what in the performance worked well. Asking students to use structures such as "I notice" or "I wonder" or "1 affirmation" and "1 challenge" can be helpful for this process. Perhaps one of the strongest reasons to teach students to take an active role in the reflection and feedback process is that it encourages a learning community where students learn from their peers and it doesn't always have to come from the teacher. In some ways, feedback from peers is more effective.

Lesson for Exploring the Role of the Observer

> *My Journey Today* (Chapter 2)

Importance of Music

Music plays an important role in the classroom. Adding music to any activity turns it from an activity to a dance. It helps set the mood, changes the energy in the classroom, and can be used to calm the class. As music is integrated into lessons, students learn to respond to the music adjusting their tempo and actions to fit the music. It also makes the performance so much more impactful (see description of the activity *Diamonds* with music from the Civil Rights Movement in Chapter 2). Music that has lyrics in other languages other than English works well as the words of the song do not get in the way. Two great resources for music are Cirque du Soleil and Putumayo World Music.

LESSON PLANS

What Are You Doing?

Grades 2–6

Students work on basic improvisation skills in this activity: thinking on their feet and using their bodies to tell a story.

Student Learning Objective

Students will participate in a physical exercise to practice basic improvisation skills.

What You Need

- Open space

How to Do the Activity

1. Have students stand in a circle.
2. One student (student 1) starts by acting out an activity, like skiing or throwing a baseball.
3. The person on their left (student 2) says, "What are you doing?"
4. Student 1 says something other than what they are doing, like: "combing my hair."
5. Then student 2 does that action.
6. The person on their left (student 3) asks: "What are you doing?" and student 2 says something other than what they are doing.
7. Student 3 begins doing this activity.
8. This goes on until everyone around the circle has done it once.
9. The object is to be able to quickly think of something other than what they are currently doing, which can be tricky for the brain to do, but is an essential skill for doing improv.
10. Repeat, going around the circle twice. (This pushes students to get even more creative).

Helpful Hints

Encourage students to do the first thing that comes to their mind. The activity does not work if you stop and allow kids to have time to think. They might say "someone already took my idea," but just encourage them to think up a new idea. Remind students that actions need to be school appropriate.

Standards Addressed

NCAS. TH:Pr5.1.3. a. Participate in a variety of physical, vocal, and cognitive exercises that can be used in a group setting for drama/theatre work.

Sculptures

Grades K-6

Sculptures is a simple exercise that can be used as a physical warm up, to practice collaboration, to explore concepts, or as a jumping off point for creating a performance piece. Students are asked to get into groups (of any number) and create a sculpture (a frozen picture) that represents a certain word or theme.

What You Need

- Open space
- List of words or themes
- Music (optional)

Student Learning Objective

Students use physical choices to create meaning in a drama/theatre work that demonstrates understanding of figurative language and the nuances of word meaning.

How to Do the Activity

Part 1: Modeling

1. Begin by modeling what a human sculpture is (a frozen picture that represents an idea). Show a picture of a sculpture that uses humans in it (a good example for older kids is *The Depression Line* by George Segal, which relates to history, or *Family Group* by Henry Moore for younger students). Discuss how the bodies are used to make a picture to tell a story.
2. Tell students that you are going to make one group sculpture together based on a theme. It's good to start with something familiar like "wintertime" or "school life." Ask one student who has an idea to enter the stage and make a pose to represent that idea or relates to the theme. (For example, if the theme is wintertime, they might enter the stage and make a pose as if they are throwing a snowball).
3. As more students have ideas, ask them to enter the scene and either make a pose that relates to the person's pose on stage, or start a new idea. (For example, they may act like they are dodging the snowball or starting to make a snowman.)
4. Encourage students to make their sculptures visually interesting and dynamic. Challenge them to think of levels with their poses: high, low, medium, and with varied positions (just like artists do to create an engaging piece.)
5. Use this format to create sculptures based on concepts (cooperation or kindness), new cite words, or to stage various parts of a read aloud (see extension).

69

Part 2: Independent/group practice (for older students)

Students work in groups to create their own sculptures and to display the varied ways that ideas can be embodied.

1. Ask students to walk around the space without talking.
2. Explain that you will call out a number or math problem. Students then make groups of that product. (For example, 1 + 3 = ? Then students get into groups of 4.)
3. Review one of the rules of doing theater (can't hurt anyone's bodies or feelings). Therefore, grabbing friends or walking away from a person who has identified you as a partner is not ok.
4. Call out a word, theme, or concept: (kindness, fear, or try a metaphor like Shakespeare's "All the worlds a stage and all the men and women merely players." Students must work together to make a sculpture (or a frozen picture) that would represent that word or idea.
5. Students should be given a short amount of time to make a sculpture (about 1 minute). More time doesn't produce better work in this case.
6. Once all students have frozen, ask one group to continue to freeze and have the other students un-freeze and take a look at the sculpture. (This will reinforce quality work). Identify some aspects that make it high quality: levels, intensity of facial expressions, originality, balance, and use of levels.)

Helpful Hints

- Music can be helpful in this activity, especially as students move around the room; you can say that they have to be in groups when the music stops.

Reflection and Wrap Up

The most important use of reflection for this activity is to instill two principles:

- How the body can be used to "tell a story," so when students do this effectively, stop and reflect with students: "What story is this sculpture telling? How do we know this?"
- There are many ways to show an idea (the arts demonstrate this effectively). If all the groups created a version of a "kindness" sculpture,

they would all be different. Discuss why this is and how this impacts storytelling. Reinforce students' abilities to be creative and how there are no wrong answers, but many solutions to challenges.

Adaptations/Extension

This is a foundational skill that can be built upon to engage with:

Social studies: Make a human timeline, create a sculpture for various moments in time for a historical figure or time period (the life of Amelia Earhart, or Women Suffragettes, or the events leading up to the American Revolution.). See **Talking Tableaux** (Chapter 5) to bring sculptures to life by creating scripts with sculptures.

Literacy: Pick a few lines of poetry to stage with sculptures. Divide students into groups, giving one line of the poem to each group to create a sculpture that embodied the ideas. Read the poem with the sculptures performed as it is read.

Science: Create a sculpture of the human body or to demonstrate the scientific method.

Math: Create sculptures to embody/demonstrate the meaning of complex math terms like: greater than less than, balance, and symmetry.

Standards Addressed

CCSS.ELA-Literacy.L.3.5 Demonstrate understanding of figurative language, word relationships, and nuances in word meanings.

NCAS. TH:Pr4.1.5. b. Use physical choices to create meaning in a drama/theatre work.

Establishing a Where

Grades K-6

In this activity, students practice using their bodies to tell a story. One student acts like they are in a place and performs mime to indicate where they are. As students figure out where this student might be, they join in and act as if they are in that same location.

What You Need

• Open space

Student Learning Objective

Students create movements and gestures to tell a story in a dramatization about an imaginary place.

How to Do the Activity

1. Ask students to think about a "where," a generic place (super-market, beach, school, shopping mall, plane) that would allow for many people to be at and doing lots of different things.
2. Ask one student, who has an idea of a place, to start (keeping the location a secret).
3. They begin doing a mime of a person in that place.
4. As students get an idea of where this might be, they may join on stage and do an action of a person who also might be in this place. (Note: the goal of the game is for all players to "be" in the same place.)
5. When many students are on stage, call "freeze."
6. Ask students one at a time where they are, and then finish off by asking the original actor where they are. See if they match up.
7. Reflect and discuss.

Helpful Hint

It can be helpful for students to share their idea with you before they start the activity to ensure it will work. You can also send them onstage one at a time. Note, the goal is for all students to be acting as if they are in the same place, but it is ok if this doesn't occur. This allows for a great conversation and learning about the importance of clarity in physicalization.

Reflect and Wrap Up

- Ask students what was needed to make this activity work, i.e., that all students "end up" in the same place.
- Discuss what implications this has for the use of the body to tell a story.
- When folks didn't end up in the same place, what might have been the reason for this?

Extensions/Adaptation

For younger students: Have a list of places to play and have all students act as if they are in that place all at once. Sidecoach to help reinforce effective use of the body to tell a story, such as "Notice what Kelly is doing, she is jumping on one foot and then the other, she looks like she is playing hop-scotch. I wonder if she is on a playground."

Connection to literacy: This can be a great way to teach about setting in a story. You can choose various settings in one book, for example, in *Goldilocks and The Three Bears*, students can create the forest (making a tree, a rock, and a river) or the house (becoming chairs of different sizes or bowls of porridge).

Connection to social studies. This can be used to learn about communities. Choose locations that are part of a community (bank, hospital, school, and park) and have students act as if they are in those locations.

Standard Addressed

NCAS. TH:Cr1.1.1.c. Identify ways in which gestures and movement may be used to create or retell a story in guided drama experiences (e.g., process drama, story drama, and creative drama)

Freeze Improvisation

Grades 1–6

This activity is a great way to introduce and practice improvisation. Students work in pairs to act out a short scene. After a short time, the teacher calls "freeze," and one student replaces one of the students on stage (using the pose as a guide) and they initiate a completely new scene using that picture.

Student Learning Objective

Students create roles, imagined worlds, and improvised stories in a drama/theater work.

How to Do the Activity

1. Ask students to think of a simple scenario that two people would be "doing" like working out at a gym, playing cards, or building a sand castle. When students have an idea, ask two students to act out this activity on stage. They may speak.
2. When the action produces an interesting "picture" (the idea is to catch a physical pose that is fruitful for re-envisioning a new scene), the facilitator calls "freeze."

3. As students view this new pose, ask students: "if this was a photograph, and it is no longer the same scene/location, what else could this scene be about?" (For example, two students are acting as if they are building a sandcastle at the beach. Looking at the frozen picture, it could be, for example, two pirates digging for hidden treasures or two folks on the floor looking for their lost contacts.) The goal is to make it drastically different from the original idea.

4. When students have an idea, you choose one student to replace one of the players on stage. The new player who enters must use the same physical pose to initiate the new scene. (For example, if one person has their hand raised in the air, the new player has to assume that same pose, and use that "hand in the air" as a new action.)

5. The student who enters starts the new scene by saying something that gives a clue to what the scene is about like: "I know it's here. I want this gold!" (They can even use a pirate voice!). The other player has to figure out very quickly what is happening in this new scene and immediately play along. (Revisit the idea of "Say yes" earlier in this chapter)

Helpful Hints

It can be helpful to do a practice round where the first set of students freeze, and you ask students to share the various new places/scenes this could be. It can also be helpful if you ask students to share their idea with you first, before they enter to make sure it will work well.

Standards Addressed

NCAS. TH:Cr1.1.3.a. Create roles, imagined worlds, and improvised stories in a drama/theatre work.

Brown Bag Improv

Grades 3–6

In this fun and engaging exercise, students will create scenes with a mismatch of who, what, and where. This is a great way to introduce the idea of character, setting, and conflict as well as to allow children to experience working together to solve a problem. This is a more advanced activity and should be completed after introducing beginning improvisation games and activities.

What You Need

- Small slips of paper
- An open space to work
- A pencil or pen for each student
- Three brown bags or hats

Student Learning Objective

Students will collaborate effectively with a partner (appropriately listening and responding, and building off each other's ideas) to create an improvised story in a dramatic work.

How to Play the Game

1. Discuss with students what a *who, what,* and *where* is in a scene. (Revisit the section "Improvision 101" earlier in this chapter). Explain that it is equivalent to the characters, setting, and conflict of a story.
2. Have students each take three sheets of paper and a pencil.
3. The students should write an example of a "who" on one sheet (Note: this has to be a pair, but the pair doesn't have to match; it could be mother and daughter or dentist and astronaut. It should be generic such as president and musician instead of George Washington and Harry Styles.) On the second slip of paper, they write a "where" or location (forest, the moon, grocery store). A "what" (conflict/problem to solve) should be written on the third sheet. The "what" is the trickiest for kids to determine. Give suggestions such as, the two are stuck in an elevator and can't get out, or their foot is stuck in gum and they are late for school, or they need directions to get to their destination, but they can't understand the other person's "language." Explain that the three ideas they chose do not have to "match." For example, they may choose a "where" that has nothing to do with the "who" or "what."
4. Mark each bag with a heading: who, what, and where. Ask students to put the appropriate sheet in the appropriate bag.
5. Divide the students into pairs. Each pair should take a sheet from each bag: one who, one what, and one where.
6. The students must work with their partners to make a scene in which the who, what, and where all make sense.
7. Have each pair perform their scene. Have the audience figure out the who, what, and where of each performance.

Helpful Hints

You can provide some "what's" for the activity in effort to have the game go smoothly or create a list on the board to be used for the game. Note: the students will claim that there is NO WAY their scene can possibly work with what they have been given, but challenge them to figure out a way!

Reflect and Wrap Up

• What helped your team solve the problem of making sense of and a scene with mismatched ideas?

Standards Addressed

CCSS.ELA-Literacy.SL.3.1 Engage effectively in a range of collaborative discussions (one-on-one, in groups, and teacher-led) with diverse partners on *grade 3 topics and texts*, building on others' ideas and expressing their own clearly.

NCAS. TH:Cr1.1.3.a. Create roles, imagined worlds, and improvised stories in a drama/theatre work.

References

Cahnamann-Taylor, M., & McGovern, K. R. (2021). *Enlivening instruction with drama and improv: A guide for second language and world language teachers*. Routledge.

Cook, S. W., Mitchell, A., & Goldin-Meadow, S. (2008). Gesturing makes learning last. *Cognition, 106*(2), 1047–1058. https://doi.org/10.1016/j.cognition.2007.04.010

Eisner, E. (2002). *The arts and the creation of mind*. Yale University Press.

Gerofsky, S. (2011). Seeing the graph vs. being the graph: Gesture, engagement and awareness in school mathematics. In G. Stam, & M. Ishino (Eds.), *Integrating gestures* (pp. 245–256). John Benjamins Publishing.

Glenberg, A. (2008). Embodiment for education. In P. Calvo, & T. Gomila (Eds.), *Handbook of cognitive science: An embodied approach* (pp. 355–372). Elsevier.

Glenberg, A. (2014, July 22). How acting in schools boosts learning: insights from embodied cognition. *Scientific American*. https://www.scientificamerican.com/article/how-acting-out-in-school-boosts-learning/

Glenberg, A., Gutierrez, T., Levin, J., Japuntich, S., & Kaschak, M. P. (2004). Activity and imagined activity can enhance young children's reading comprehension. *Journal of Educational Psychology, 96*(3), 424–436.

Goldberg, M. (2021). *Arts integration: Teaching subject matter through the arts in multicultural settings* (6th ed.). Routledge.

Hardiman, M. (2012). *Brain targeted teaching model for 21st-century schools.* Corwin Press.

Johnson-Glenberg, M. C., Birchfield, D. A., Tolentino, L., & Koziupa, T. (2014). Collaborative embodied learning in mixed reality motion-capture environments: Two science studies. *Journal of Educational Psychology, 106*(1), 86–104.

Kelly, S. D., McDevitt, T., & Esch, M. (2009). Brief training with co-speech gesture lends a hand to word learning in a foreign language. *Language and Cognitive Processes, 24*(2), 313–334.

Noice, H., & Noice, T. (2013). Extending the reach of an evidence-based theatrical intervention. *Experimental Aging Research, 39*(4), 398–418. https://doi.org/10.1080/0361073X.2013.808116

Petrick, C. J. (2012). *Every body move: Learning mathematics through embodied actions.* (Doctoral dissertation, University of Texas).

Roth, W. M. (2001). Gestures: Their role in teaching and learning. *Review of Education Research, 71*(3), 365–392.

Shapiro, L., & Stolz, S. A. (2019). Embodied cognition and its significance for education. *Theory and Research in Education, 17*(1), 19–39. https://doi.org/10.1177/1477878518822149

Spolin, V. (1963). *Improvisation for the theater: A handbook of teaching and directing techniques* (1st ed.). Northwestern University Press.

Spolin, V. (1986). *Theater games for the classroom: A teacher's handbook.* Northwestern University Press.

Leaping for Literacy

Picture This....

I am working with a class called STEP (Studying Toward English Proficiency) at the Integrated Arts Academy. This is a small group of students who have recently moved to the United States and are of varying ages, speak various languages, and have limited English language proficiency. The activity for the day is **Letter Dance** (see Box 4.1 for full description) where students are tasked with working with a partner to spell their names using their bodies. The activity has a variety of parts. First, I pair students with someone they don't know well. Then, they are tasked with spelling both of their names by making letters together using their bodies (see Figure 4.1). They finish by performing for their peers, who work to "read" the names and figure out which name is being performed. Working with this group, I decided that we needed to adapt this activity to help students be successful. Instead of each pair working on their own names, we decided to spell all of the students' names in the class, having all the pairs work on one name at the same time. The students quickly came alive. Even the older student jumped right in who typically had issues with participation (and who could blame her, she was 3 grades older than the rest of the group and likely didn't want to be there!) This adaptation of the activity worked extremely well. The student whose name was being spelled was so excited to have their classmates working on and saying their name, and the other students were thrilled to be moving, working with a partner, and communicating. We couldn't speak the same language for the most part, but we could all repeat the person's name, and the students started to say letter names, like "a...a?!"

DOI: 10.4324/9781003296317-4

Letter Dance

Letter dance is an excellent introductory activity for integrating movement into a literacy lesson while building classroom community! Students are paired with someone they don't know well. They are tasked with making the letters of their names (one at a time), using their bodies. For example, if they are making the letter "I," they need to find a way for this to be created as a team. So one student might be the straight line and the other one might use their hands to make the dot (see Figure 4.1 of students making an "i" during *Letter Dance*). Once students have been given some time to make their names, task them with turning it into a "dance." To accomplish this, ask them to choose one of the two names to work on and find a way to move from one letter to the next, making it a fun and smooth transition. Students perform their names for their classmates, and classmates guess which name is being performed. At the end of the lesson, ask for all the pairs who made a certain letter, like "I" to go to the "stage." It is a great learning lesson to see all the varied ways students chose to make their letter, which reinforces the power of creativity and that there are lots of ways to solve a problem!

Box 4.1 Description of *Letter Dance* Activity

in effort to communicate that they had made an A. The classroom teacher was thrilled with this class session, and I was too. It was a reminder of the power of the arts to create a space for all students to get involved. Since many of the activities are movement focused, they depend less on verbal communication, so students can feel immediately included and experience success! This is why activities like this that utilize drama and movement can improve learning outcomes students who are ELs (Brouillette et al., 2014; Cahnamann-Taylor & McGovern, 2021; Greenfader & Brouillette, 2014). Students who have limited English language proficiency can not only fully participate in the instruction, they can take center stage!

Letter Dance is a successful literacy lesson in any classroom. Look at how many things that are accomplished in one short activity:

- Students practice collaboration as they work with a peer to accomplish the task

Figure 4.1 Students participating in **Letter Dance**
(Photo taken by author with permission from IAA)

- Bridges are made in the class as students are encouraged to work with someone they don't know well
- Students learn each other's names which builds classroom community
- Students practice making their letters
- Students practice reading and identifying letters
- Students practice providing feedback as they act as active observers
- Students see that there are multiple ways to solve a problem which is reinforced as all students share the varied ways they make a letter
- Students develop their imaginations and build skills in creativity as they explore ways to create a movement piece

Letter Dance exemplifies the powerful punch using movement and theater has on a literacy lesson. This chapter will explore more ways in which theater and dance can be integrated with literacy to make your classroom a vibrant, engaging, and active space for deeper learning for all students.

Research on the Benefits of Integrating Movement and Theater with Literacy

Movement, drama, and dance are effective vehicles for literacy development and another way to differentiate instruction for students. If we understand arts integration as defined by Diaz, Donovan, and Pascale, as an "avenue for rigorous investigation, representation, expression, and reflection of both curricular content and the art form itself" (Donovan & Pascale, 2012, p. 14), then using theater or movement in a literacy lesson is an optimal way for students to engage with a text. It allows for varied avenues for students to explore ideas, construct meaning, and share their understanding in alternative ways, not always relying on one form of communication (speaking or writing).

There is some promising research that supports the notion that theater and movement are effective way to increase literacy skills. Chisholm and Whitmore's (2016) found that arts-integrated and embodied learning opportunities supported students' sensemaking about complex narratives. Brouillette et al. (2014) in their study of the outcomes of the Teaching Artist Project (TAP) at five large urban elementary schools in San Diego found that integrating drama activities into literacy work supported oral language development for kindergarteners and students who are ELs because it provided rich opportunities for verbal interaction between teachers and pupils. Mages' (2006) study supports drama's effect on the narrative development of very young children (ages 2–7) specifically children's oral storytelling and aural comprehension.

Maximizing Learning with Multiliteracies

While the definition of literacy has traditionally been thought of as reading, writing, and numeracy, some would argue this concept should be expanded considering the highly globalized and increasingly visual and digital reality of the 21st century. The London Group, a group of researchers and practitioners, coined the term multiliteracies in 1996 (Cazden et al., 1996). They argue that our current definition of literacy is grounded in the written word which misses the multifaceted ways we communicate now in our highly globalized, technology-driven, visually stimulated, more culturally and linguistically diverse world. This new conception of literacy expands the previous definition to ensure that differences in gender, culture, and language are not barriers to educational and work success. UNESCO supports this expanded understanding of literacy, suggesting it should be more broadly understood as a means to understand, interpret, create, and communicate.

Multiliteracies could include the use of the body or visuals as alternative forms of communication which encourages varied engagement with a text, creating more space for cultural and linguistic diversity (Cahnamann-Taylor & McGovern, 2021; Gilbert, 2002). Anne Green Gilbert (2002) in her book *Teaching the Three Rs* affirms that movement exploration provides students who lack strong verbal skills a chance to express themselves, helping these students to be more successful in the classroom. Providing learning grounded in movement also ensures students who are ELs a better way to access and share their thinking (Chahnamann-Taylor & McGovern, 2021). Eileen Landay and Kurt Wootton (2012) are utilizing the notion of multiliteracies in The ArtsLiteracy Project which uses their framework, *The Performance Cycle*, to encourage students to use theater techniques to comprehend, perform, and reflect on a text. They argue that literacy goes beyond comprehending printed texts and that the arts can help to bridge a text with students' lives, which is essential for caring about and understanding a literary work.

Using a Multimodal Approach to ELA

Multimodality means that students are provided with a variety of ways to engage in the learning process to make meaning, beyond the spoken and written word. This could include the use of dance, images, music, and gestures to name a few. Chisholm and Whitmore (2016) found that a multimodal approach increased learning for middle school students about *Anne Frank: The Diary of a Young Girl* and also encouraged empathy. A multimodal approach has proven to increase access to content, help to generate more insights, and allow students to share their understanding in different ways (Chisholm & Whitmore, 2016). Peggy Albers (2006) argues that a multimodal approach to teaching literacy is paramount considering the changes due to technology that require students to read and interpret a multitude of varied texts, communication styles, and images. Additionally, a multimodal perspective "values the lives and experience that learners bring to English Language Arts classrooms" and has the power to communicate more complex meaning (Albers, 2006, p. 76).

Transmediation and Literacy

There is a connection between multimodal approaches to learning and transmediation. While transmediation was discussed in earlier chapters to explore why arts integration is an effective pedagogy, it is also important to reiterate its benefits for literacy development. Transmediation is the act of transferring meaning from one sign system to another in effort to generate new understandings (Fattal, 2019). This occurs when multimodal approaches are used in the classroom, for example, using music to respond to a written text. Harste (2014) suggests an example of transmediation is "the process of taking what one knows in language and representing it in art" (p. 88). Fattal (2019) researched the effects of transmediation on both language development and content knowledge in multiple bilingual elementary education classrooms. She argues that the benefit of transmediation is that, "creating meaning in a second sign system forces the student to reexamine the central concept of the original composition" (Fattal, 2019, p. 88). Many of the activities in this book require students to transfer meaning to another sign system such as movement or theater and in doing so encourages deeper learning.

What Might This Look Like in a Classroom?

Let's revisit the *My Journey Today* activity that was shared in Chapter 2 to explore how this works. This exercise requires students to act out their day, without speaking, using only their bodies. Students might start by laying down on the floor pretending to wake up, then act as if getting dressed or brushing their teeth and show their trip to school. If this exercise is used in a literacy lesson, it could offer a multimodal approach to engaging with a text. If you were reading *Little Red Riding Hood*, students could be asked to act out Red's journey in the story. Students might show packing the picnic, putting on their cape, and walking through the woods. They might show walking faster as they hear scary sounds or stopping to talk to the wolf. They might mimic knocking on the door of their grandmother's house and running home after seeing the wolf in grandma's clothing. After a rehearsal, students could perform for each other and be asked to share if any of the movements they see represent what they read in the book.

This is an example of transmediation because the students are transferring the written word into physical movements, one sign system to another. This process takes critical thinking skills as the student must first think of what they read and then figure out how to show it with their bodies (without speaking). Not only is there a benefit of this process as students perform, but also in their role as observer. As students look for evidence in their classmates' performance of what they know of the story, the concepts, ideas, and details can be recounted offering an opportunity to reinforce the learning for all. The rest of the chapter shares a variety of ways that you can use a multimodal approach to teaching literacy.

Storytelling and Theater

Oral storytelling is an age-old artform, predating the written word. Many stories around the world have been passed down through oral traditions. Storytelling is an excellent way for students to practice creating stories before they write them down. It can be used to improve students' ability to expand on ideas and to practice public speaking skills. Storytelling can also encourage movement in the learning process, as an engaging storyteller uses gestures and often some physical movements to entertain their audience. Brouillette (2019) argues that children telling their own stories is a means by which students practice basic literacy skills in a way that garners student enthusiasm that might not be equally present during regular school day lessons. Storytelling provides a rich learning experience for students, perhaps bridging experiences from home to school, potentially expanding students' cultural experiences and understanding which helps to build community.

An Example of Using Storytelling in Your Classroom

Imagine instead of the typical share during morning meeting, you ask your students to think about any event that happened to them recently that they would like to recount for the class. It could be their harrowing trip to school that day or something that happened the night before like the worst dinner ever or how they lost their soccer game in overtime. It is important to explain that the story doesn't have to be funny or "earth shattering," but simply the act of sharing details of an event that happened to them no matter how big or small. What you will notice is that some students might tell a 30-second story and some a more detailed and longer one. Be sure to reinforce that all stories are equally acceptable (as long as it is school appropriate). You can do this by modeling how this is done by making your example very succinct and not too dramatic (setting the bar low to start). You can also reinforce the acceptability of any story with your feedback. It is important, however, to make sure the stories aren't too long, perhaps capping it around 3 minutes, to ensure engagement for all. A timer can be helpful for doing this. If you have introduced the concept of a *small moment* (Calkins, 2020) in your literacy class, this is a great connection to make to better articulate the goal of expanding one moment into a rich and detailed story. Be sure to tell students to be active listeners, listening for elements in the story like who, what, and where as they will be asked to recount the stories later.

When all students (or perhaps a few for that day) have gone, explain that they are going to retell a story that has been already told, but from a new *perspective*. Ask students if there is another character in one of the stories they heard that they can tell the story from their point of view. For example, for the student who tells the story about the ending of their soccer game from their perspective, could they tell it from the perspective of someone on the other team? Explain that their job is to recount as many details of the story as possible (without revealing which story they are telling). It is ok to add additional elements that might be necessary to tell the event from the other characters' perspective. One of the most creative examples of story retelling was when one student shared about taking their dog for a walk and all the people they met on the way. In the retelling, a student told it from the perspective of the dog. You may be thinking, "my kids can't do this, it's too complicated!" But these stories can be very simple and short, and with practice, you'd be surprised how well your students can handle this challenge.

Teaching Perspective

This storytelling activity is an excellent way to teach the concept of perspective. It allows students to see how changing the view of an event can change its meaning. It also allows students to practice seeing an event from a different point of view. This storytelling activity also helps students understand the idea of "audience" and that each story (oral or written) is for the benefit of sharing. Having an audience who reacts in real time can push students to expand more on their story (giving even more details) or increase their expression. Additionally, having students all model the storytelling activity allows them to learn from their peers and see lots of varied examples. Sharing exemplars is not as easy when it comes to sharing students' writing because it can take longer for students to get to a place where their writing is ready to share. Storytelling gets students to share earlier in the process which benefits all. Most importantly, storytelling helps students practice using their *imagination,* which is essential for any writer!

Storytelling and Writing

This storytelling activity demonstrates a plethora of ways that oral storytelling connects to literacy development and can be used to teach some key concepts about writing in a more active and engaging way. Here are a few examples:

- *Exploring small moments*: Lucy Calkins, a leader in writing programs for schools, has developed the idea of "small moments" as a step in teaching the writing of personal narratives. She encourages young writers to focus less on a big event and more on a small one, adding lots of details, description, and character development to hook the reader. This storytelling activity helps students practice this skill because, in the act of telling, it is almost impossible not to have the characters come to life with details. Having an audience also encourages students to be even more descriptive in effort to captivate their audience.

- *Elements of a story*: Teaching elements of a story (who, what, where) is part of most literacy programs in US elementary schools. The Common Core ELA standards cover a variety of standards for building skills in this area. These benchmarks can be easily modeled with this storytelling activity in a more engaging way because it starts with the students' personal stories. Perhaps choose one story told that day and ask: *Who* are the characters in the story? *What* were the events? *Where* was the story set? Was there any moral to the story or lesson learned by the main character? If you start with their stories, you are likely to get more buy in.

- *Sequencing*: Another skill required for reading comprehension is sequencing. This activity helps to teach students this skill. By having the re-teller retell the parts of the story in order, even from a different viewpoint, the student is both practicing and demonstrating the skill of sequencing.

- *Reading with expression*: Perhaps one of the best skills that can be taught through storytelling is speaking with expression. To grab the audience's attention, storytellers need to vary their range, volume, and express their emotions in a way that communicates with the audience. Having an audience who provides real-time feedback encourages the storyteller to get even more expressive.

Storytelling is a great way to start the process of expression (both vocally and physically in your classroom). Integrating other theater techniques can expand upon this skill and take learning to new heights!

Integrating Theater into Your Literacy Lessons

Reader as Actor

At the heart of literacy is stories told by people from all walks of life, recounting major events and the journeys taken to either learning or transformation. Theater has the same goal of telling stories, but it goes beyond the written word. In theater, there are a multitude of layers that add meaning to the original text or script, which makes it an excellent tool for deepening students' learning in literacy. The first layer is a script, or the written word. In general, when we read books, the text is the "end" of the process, but in plays, the script is the beginning of the storytelling. The script is then utilized by directors who make choices about the setting and the way the story will be told and actors who add their interpretation to text with the way they perform the lines. Actors use inflection and expression that adds more dimension and perhaps alternative meaning to what is written on the page. This first step demonstrates the way in which engaging acting in your lessons can boost literacy development, encouraging students to engage more deeply with the text in effort to make some dramatic choices (see Figure 4.2 as students create their own poses in a literacy class).

In effort to demonstrate this idea for students, try this **interpretation activity**. On the board or cards write the lines:

What time is it?
The time is near.

Then ask students to work in pairs to stage this scene. They must decide on *who* are the characters in the scene, *where* the scene takes place, and *what* the "problem" is that the characters are trying to solve (revisit Chapter 3, "Improvisation 101: Establishing the *Who, What, Where*".) The performances shared by students will be as varied as the number of pairs in your classroom. One group might make it about two students who are late for class. One student might walk over to the desk of the other student and ask "what time is it?" referring to how much time there is until their next class. The other student might point at their watch and answer: "the time is near," as if they mean, it's almost time to go. Then they both jump up and walk quickly as if rushing to class. Perhaps another pair's performance is more grave and they play a person sitting on the edge of a hospital bed. They might turn to the "doctor" and ask "what time is it?" meaning how much longer, and the doctor answers with a shake of his head "the time is near," as if to communicate there isn't much time until the patient passes. A last group might make their scene about astronauts, both sitting in their rocket ship. One turns to their

Figure 4.2 Students use their bodies to create a pose in a literacy lesson.
(Photograph taken by author with permission from IAA)

co-pilot with an excited tone and asks: "what time is it?" demonstrating their excitement for what is about to happen. And after the other actor professes: "The time is near," they begin to shake as if the rocket engine is beginning its take off.

This exercise demonstrates a multitude of ways that the *reader as actor* can shape the meaning of a piece of literature, encouraging students to dig deeper into texts:

- *Expression*: The way the actor says the line can alter the meaning of a text and have a big impact on how the text is understood. Having students read sections of a text that are in quotes, meaning they are intended to be "spoken" by characters in a story, as an actor would, will get children practicing reading with expression and help them better understand how inflection can alter the meaning of a text.

- *Physicalization*: Adding gestures or movement can change the meaning of the text. For example, the actor who plays the anxious student in the previous exercise may look at their watch or pace, communicating they are nervous about the time and what's to come. However, if this actor chose instead to lay his forehead on his desk and barely raise his head as he asks this same question, it communicates something entirely different. Try taking a few lines from a text you are reading and ask students to vary the way they physicalize them. Discuss how choices for how the text is staged may add to or alter meaning.

- *Actor's choices*: In acting terms, this means the way in which the actor interprets the meaning of the text and thus chooses to "play" it be it physically or vocally. This notion is a powerful learning tool in the classroom. Giving students opportunities to make different choices of how to play, and thus interpret a scene, lays the foundation for rich discussions about text meaning and inferences.

- *Inferences* are making a guess at meaning that is not explicitly shared in a written text. It is often deemed, "reading between the lines." It can be what is happening either physically or emo-tionally, but perhaps not explicit in what the character says, yet is foundational to interpreting the scene. Goldberg (2021) shares that the notion of inference is difficult for many readers and that theater is an optimal way to teach this skill. By "becoming the character, students gain insight into a character's thoughts, actions, and motivations, thus providing an opening for students to enter into a deeper understanding of the text" (Goldberg, 2021, p. 82).

Dramatizing a Scene from Your Read Aloud

Try staging a scene from a chapter book or read aloud to help students dive more deeply into the text using theater techniques. Prior to working with students, turn a few pages of the book into a script, using only the words that are in quotation marks (as they are meant to be spoken) and writing them next to the characters names. An example of how this can be done is shared below, using a selection from the book *Wonder* (2012), a book that is often read in 5th grade. This is a great scene to act out in your classroom as it takes place in a school and the characters are school age, so your students should have a pretty easy time taking on these roles.

Staging *Wonder*, Chapter: "Jack Will, Julian, and Charlotte,"
(Palacio, 2012 pp. 21–22)

The section starts with the principal Mr. Tushman introducing Jack, a new student at school (bottom of p. 21). It is a typical scene you might see in any school. While this may seem like a pretty pedestrian conversation, it is one that young students can easily relate to as "the new kid in school routine." Students can likely empathize with both sides of this exchange, perhaps as the new kid or the veteran welcoming a new student. This scene provides a great entry point into both practicing inference and experiencing the impact that "reader and actor" has on the meaning of a text.

- **Place students into groups** of 4. Ask them to choose *who* they will play, regardless of gender. If need be, change the names to: Principal, "C," "J," and "J.W." Tell students that they are going to take the scene out of context and try to "play" it with a variety of "whats" (review Chapter 3: "Improvisation 101: *Establishing Who, Where, What"*).
  1. If need be, suggest or **assign** some potential "whats":
     - The kids are all super excited to meet a new student
     - Students are not at all excited to meet a new student
     - Some are excited and some are not
- Before sending students off to rehearse, discuss this last possible scenario ("some are excited and some are not") for validity. Tell them before actors make choices in how they will play a scene, they dig

into the text for clues! What clues can be found to support this last "choice" for how it is performed? Looking at the text more closely, the reader will see that the author describes some of Jack Will's body language during the introduction. He "half smiled" as he took Auggie's hand, and after shaking it, "looked down really fast." Will "forced" a smile (as perceived by Auggie) and also "looked down fast." While Charlotte gave a quick wave and smile and offered more than just a "hey."

- Have students **rehearse** their scene based on the interpretation they chose?
- Have students **perform** for the class?
- **Discuss**
  - Did all the ways this scene was played out work?
  - Which one do you think more closely aligned with the author's intent? Why or why not.

Taking the time to dramatize a scene from a text you are reading will teach so much more than rushing through a reading and having a quick discussion. Students will be 100% active and engaged in the learning and have a deeper understanding of the text. In this example, students will have a better understanding of the challenges that Augie faces going to school. They might also make a stronger connection to both the theme or the characters by taking on the roles in this way. This might even help students learn some empathy. If you have younger students, try using sculptures to bring a text to life using theater (see Box 4.2).

Staging a Read Aloud Using Sculptures

Choose a read aloud story that has lots of action! Pick an image that can be recreated with a sculpture for each page. Put students in groups of 4, giving each group one page of the story or image to recreate using a group pose. Students work as a group to figure out how to create a sculpture to represent the action on their page. Facilitate and coach as students work. Bring students back. As you read the story aloud, ask each group to stand and share their sculpture as their page is read aloud.

Box 4.2 Describes How to Use Sculptures *in a Literacy Lesson*

Staging a Fable or Folktale

Staging a folktale or fable can be a great way to engage in literacy development (see Figure 4.3, students staging of *Where the Wild Things Are*). It can also be an excellent way to explore learning about other cultures. Johnny Saldaña (1995) a leader in the field of what he calls "multiethnic education," suggests that dramatizing folklore is a "springboard for examining different ethnic perspectives and worldviews" (p. xii). (See *Drama of Color* for more ways to dramatize folklore). An excellent fable for staging is *Why the Sun and the Moon Live in the Sky* written by Elphinstone Dayrell (1990) and illustrated by Blair Lent. It is a Nigerian fable that explains the mystery of how the sun and moon came to be in the sky. The illustrations are gorgeous and provide a lot of inspiration for integrating the arts and movement into a literacy lesson.

One of the challenges to staging a story is how to "cast" it. For example, should one student play the sun and one play the moon as would likely be done if you were putting on a play? Instead, have groups of students each act out one page of the story. This way, there will be a multitude of students

Figure 4.3 Children presented their staging of the book *Where the Wild Things Are*

who play sun and moon. The illustrations in the story show the characters wearing masks. If you end up performing this fable for your school or community, consider creating masks for the sun and moon that can be shared between players to help the audience follow the story more easily (see Box 4.3 about mask making and cultural responsiveness).

Step by Step Staging of a Folktale

- **Make a copy** of each of the pages, being sure to write a number on each so you can perform it in order later.
- **Assign** three or four students to each page.
- Have students **Establish the Who, What, Where** (see Chapter 3 for review of this process).
- Students **decide who will play which part**. Note: This can be challenging because not every scene (page of the text) breaks down perfectly

Creation and Use of Masks: Being Culturally Responsive

Mask-making is a great way to integrate the arts into a lesson, to learn about another culture, and create workable costumes for a performance. *Why the Sun and the Moon Live in the Sky,* which depicts masks in the illustrations of this tale, offers entry into a study on the use of masks in other cultures. While masks are used all over the world, and often in Theater productions, it is important to provide both the context and historical and cultural significance for mask wearing. Since this is a fable from Nigeria, provide some background knowledge on the use of masks in Nigeria. Teach your students that masks are often used for ceremonies and rituals and have religions and spiritual meaning. They are also specially made by artists and have important prominence in their culture. Therefore, when creating masks, first explore their history and cultural significance and view some of the masks that have been created by Nigerian artists. Creating masks with your students would greatly add to the performance of *Why the Sun and the Moon Live in the Sky.* Paper plates work great for mask making (see Figure 4.4). However, be sure to clarify that your masks are *inspired by* Nigerian masks, not intended to mimic. Making this clear will help teach students gain respect for other culture's important traditions. This could also lead to a discussion of cultural appropriation.

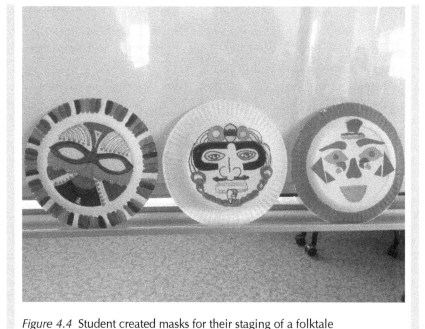

Figure 4.4 Student created masks for their staging of a folktale

Box 4.3 Describes How to Include Masks Making in Your Staging of a Folktale While Being Culturally Responsive.

into three or four players. However, this is where critical thinking comes in! When students run to you and inform you that either (a) they don't have enough parts, (b) there aren't enough parts for all, or (c) they have too many parts and need more students, you respond with: "I know you can solve this problem and figure out how to make it work." Trust me, they always do.

- Ask students to **underline any of the sentences** that could be spoken by a character; this becomes their script.
- Have them **circle any physical activity** that could be used in their staging.
- If they have a hard time getting started, have them **create a sculpture**. Then one student starts by saying something like what their character in the pose might say. Then, have each of the other students respond to this statement. For example, if students are in a pose with sun and moon inside the house, *Sun* could start by saying something like:

"Wow this house is really nice!" Then ask *Moon* to respond and then maybe the *House*. This often is just the start kids need to get things moving (see *Talking Tableaux*, Chapter 5, for more details on how to create scenes from sculptures).

- **Present** each of the scenes for their peers. Ask students to offer some critical **feedback** that will help the groups make their scene even stronger using either "I notice" or "I wonder" or offering one acknowledgment and one challenge. Remind them that theater is about telling a story to the audience. If the audience has any confusion about what is happening, that may be a place to revise and rethink in their next rehearsal.
- Have students take feedback and **rehearse again**. This step of the process is very important. When pressed for time, it can be easy to omit. However, this part of the process offers so many valuable learning opportunities for your students:
  - Models that art also needs revisions which reinforces the notion that work goes into creating something ready to be "shared."
  - Offers a chance to make a connection to writing; just like a writer gets feedback and makes revisions, same for artists who create a work of art.
  - Teaches grit and perseverance.
  - Provides practice in critical thinking skills: challenging students to figure out how to address the audiences' feedback to make it even more clear for the audience.
- **Perform**: It's showtime: End the class or unit with a performance, be it for your class or school community.
- *Add Music*: Find some Nigerian music to use for transitions. It will make it feel even more like a performance and set the mood.
- *Dance*: This story has many opportunities for adding a dance, especially as more and more friends come to the Sun's house making the water continue to rise. Try creating a short dance that can demonstrate this with movement. Don't want to figure this out yourself? Have your students create the choreography. Have each group work to create a movement piece that demonstrates the rising waters with movement. Pick one group's rendition (that works best) and have them teach it to the whole class so all can participate in this dance.

LESSON PLANS FOR INTEGRATING THEATER AND DANCE WITH ELA

Verb Dance

Grades 3–6

Students use this fun and movement-filled activity to embody new vocabulary words, with particular attention to action verbs. Students choose an action verb, perform it, and participate in a collaborative creative experience. This can be used in a literacy lesson, as a morning meeting activity, or to practice spatial awareness and moving safely.

What You Need

- Card stock—one for each student
- Magic markers
- Action verbs (created through a brainstorm session or by each student thinking of one on their own)
- An open space to work
- Music

Student Learning Objective

Students will create movements that express an idea and act out the meaning of verbs that are differing in manner.

How to Do the Activity

1. Ask students if they can define an action verb.
2. Ask each student to name an action verb: a verb that calls for action (movement) and write one action verb in large letters (so it is able to be read from a distance) on a piece of cardstock.
3. Ask students to sit in a large circle and place their card face down in front of them.
4. Play music.
5. Begin by asking one or two students to start the action as "movers." They are to walk toward another student. As the moving student approaches another student, the seated player must hold up their card so it can be read. The mover then finds a way to use their body

to express the verb written on the card. (For example, the word may be wiggle, and the mover will shake their whole body, swinging their arms forward and back.) The mover does this motion across the circle to another student and repeats this process with a new seated player.

6. Once the mover acts out three verbs, they will tap another student on the shoulder and switch places with them. They sit behind the card of their classmate and that classmate becomes the new mover.

7. When the teachers feel it is time, and the class is moving safely around the circle, more movers may be added to the circle.

Hints for Success

Music choice is key for the success of this activity. An uptempo piece is preferred, which encourages more energy from students. Additionally, If students can't think of action verbs themselves, brainstorm a list of verbs that can be used prior to playing.

Reflection and Wrap Up

• Ask students to define an action verb now—and if their definition or meaning of this idea is more clear after this exercise.

• What did they notice about the activity or their peers' work? (This is often where students notice that there were varied ways to embody some of the words, which reinforces how people can interpret words differently and that words can have different meanings.)

Adaptation for Younger Grades (K-2)

Brainstorm a list of action words together or you can provide simple action verbs on cards such as jump, hop, roll, walk (with pictures if using for kindergarten.) Hold up each card one at a time and ask all students to "read" and do the actions together.

Standards Addressed

CCSS.ELA-Literacy.L.1.5d Distinguish shades of meaning among verbs differing in manner (e.g., *look, peek, glance, stare, glare, scowl*) by defining or choosing them or by acting out the meanings.

NCAS. Creating: Core Standard #2: Organize and develop artistic ideas and work; DA.CR.2.1.1: b. Choose movements that express an idea or emotion or follow a musical phrase.

Choral Reading

Grades 1–6

In this activity, the entire class will work together to read and create motions to express a poem or passage of literature. The activity can be used to begin a poetry unit, a means of memorizing material, or to warm up bodies and voices before starting the day. It can also be used to teach about homophones as students will naturally act out different meanings to words. This is a great introduction activity because all the students are working at the same time; no one child is put on the spot or has to perform alone in front of their peers.

What You Need

- A piece of literature: poem or short paragraph with lots of repetitive words written on a poster board or board
- An open space

Student Learning Objective

Students will determine the meaning of words and phrases as they are used in a text, generating ideas, and using gestures to retell the story.

How to Do the Activity

(This is explained as if you were using the poem, *Pie Problem* by Shel Silverstein, 1981)

1. Explain the origin of the term "chorus," that in theatrical performances in Ancient Greece, they had a group of people that would speak and move together (called a chorus). Their job was to tell the audience what was happening in the plot. Students will become a chorus in this activity.
2. Work through the poem one word (or short phrase at a time).
3. With each word, ask all the students to make a move that expresses what the word means to them.
4. You will pick one of the actions that you will "use" moving forward. (I usually don't say the persons' name, but something like, "A lot of people are pointing to themselves to enact the word 'I,' so let's do that action for that word."

5. Do this with each word as you progress through the passage. When you get to a word that repeats, simply do the action you have already agreed upon for this word.

6. When you come to a homophone, like "so," often there will be children who will make an action as if to "sew." I stop at this point and discuss the meaning of a homophone.

7. As you finish a section of the piece, either a line or a few lines, go back and review-performing what you have created so far all together

8. When you get to a punctuation mark, this is another opportunity to have a short discussion. For example, when you get to a period, a student may put their hand out as if to motion "stop" like a traffic guard might do. This leads to a great discussion that a period does mean to stop. When you get to an exclamation point, you may have a student say you need to make the action prior to the punctuation even more dramatic or you may have the students jump up and throw their arms in the air as if making an exclamation point. Both actions exemplify what the punctuation wants the speaker or reader to do, which is to add emphasis.

9. Continue to review as you move through the piece.

10. Finish by performing the entire piece together.

Extensions or Adaptations

You can use any short poem or piece of literature for this exercise or make up actions to go with a poem you have created in your class based on other learning. Hint: The activity works much better with a short selection that has a lot of repetition.

Standards Addressed

CCSS.ELA-Literacy.RL.3.4 Determine the meaning of words and phrases as they are used in a text, distinguishing literal from nonliteral language.

CCSS.ELA-LITERACY.CCRA.L.5 Demonstrate understanding of figurative language, word relationships, and nuances in word meanings.

NCAS. Theater: Anchor Standard 1: Generate and conceptualize artistic ideas and work. TH:Cr1.1.1.c-Identify ways in which gestures and movement may be used to create or retell a story in guided drama experiences (e.g., process drama, story drama, creative drama).

Adverb Walk

Grades K-6

Adverb Walk is a fun and engaging way to get your kids up and moving and demonstrating adverbs. Students can experience how adding descriptive language, such as adverbs, changes the meaning, and/or the intensity of a verb.

What You Need

- An open space
- A board to list adverbs
- Music

Student Learning Objective

Select and apply appropriate characteristics to movements (i.e., specific adverbs) that demonstrate and clarify the meaning of unknown words.

How to Do the Activity

- Ask the students to define an adverb (or have them name all the ways you can "walk")
- Make a list of these adverbs on the board (explaining they will be used to more fully describe how they will "walk" in this exercise).
- Play music
- Have students move around the space
- When you stop the music, call out an adverb, such as "quickly." Direct students to interpret that word and thus walk in a way that exemplifies the meaning of that adverb.
- Play the game with 8 to 10 adverbs

Reflect and Wrap Up

- How did the adverb change the way you walked?
- What is an adverb? (See if how they define adverbs has changed.)
- What might adverbs do to your writing?

Extension or Adaptation

- You can also accomplish this by having students walk one at a time across the circle toward another player; then switch places with that student to switch turns. This can be used as a morning meeting greeting.

- Use this same format to enhance a study of modes of travel (such as fly, drive, swim,) or you may use this same format and use action verbs to promote movement (leap, skip, roll, slide, jump, etc.)

Standards Addressed

CCSS.ELA-LITERACY.CCRA.L.4 Determine or clarify the meaning of unknown and multiple-meaning words and phrases by using context clues, analyzing meaningful word parts, and consulting general and specialized reference materials, as appropriate.

NCAS. Dance: Performing Anchor Standard 4: Select, analyze, and interpret artistic work for presentation. Select and apply appropriate characteristics to movements (for example, selecting specific adverbs and adjectives and applying them to movements). Demonstrate kinesthetic awareness while dancing the movement characteristics.

Poetry in Motion

Grades 1–6

This simple group activity will help your students understand imagery. Using a short poem that can be divided into small sections or phrases, students can work together to create a simple movement or frozen tableaux that exemplifies the images the poet is trying to convey in their poem. This will allow students to explore a poem more deeply, work with their peers, and better understand the meaning of the poem.

What You Need

- A poem, song, or picture book with strong imagery
- Cards with the poem divided up evenly for your group of students; preferably one line or one page for each group (numbered so that the piece can be performed in order.)
- An open space

Student Learning Objective

Students will develop artistic ideas that demonstrate effective choices for meaning and stronger comprehension of a selected text.

How to Do the Activity

1. Divide the class into groups of 3 or 4 students.
2. Give each group a card from the poem (or text).
3. Explain that in poetry, there is a lot of imagery. Imagery is used by poets to create pictures in your mind and is intended to express ideas that words are hard to express.
4. Ask each group to come up with a way to "act" out the images on their card either by creating a sculpture or frozen image (see Chapter 2, *sculptures*). It is great to use Shakespeare's poem, *Winter Song,* to introduce this idea, as it talks about being *frozen*! (See selection provided). Students can also create a movement and add sound. Each group must also decide on how they will say their line of the poem. The group may choose to have one speaker say the line in unison or divide the lines up and have various speakers.
5. Have each group perform their piece in order, performing the entire poem as a class.
6. If time allows, have each group perform first, having classmates offer feedback, allowing for a second rehearsal before performing the final piece.

Reflect and Wrap Up

*   What did creating a tableaux or movements to demonstrate meaning in the text do for your understanding of the poem?
*   What is imagery?
*   How does imagery impact writing?

Poetry Selection

Icicles, Shakespeare's *Winter Song* from *Love's Labour's Lost*

(Note: A poem from Shakespeare is used as an example as it is free domain, see examples below for ways to use more diverse texts in your classroom).

1
When icicles hang by the wall,
2
And Dick the shepherd blows his nail,
3
And Tom bears longs into the hall,

4
And milk comes frozen home in pail
5
When blood is nipp'd and ways be foul,
6
The nightly sings the staring owl,
7
Tu-whit, Tu-who, a merry note,
8
While greasy Joan doth keel the pot

Expansions or Adaptations

For younger students: Try Shel Silverstein's *Bear in My Frigidaire*

For older students: Try Langston Hughes' *Dreams* or Amanda Gorman's *The Hill We Climb*

Standards Addressed

CCSS. Knowledge of Language: CCSS.ELA-LITERACY.CCRA.L.3. Apply knowledge of language to understand how language functions in different contexts, to make effective choices for meaning or style, and to comprehend more fully when reading or listening.

NCAS. Theater: Anchor Standard 1: Generate and conceptualize artistic ideas and work. TH:Cr1.1.1.c-Identify ways in which gestures and movement may be used to create or retell a story in guided drama experiences (e.g., process drama, story drama, creative drama).

Vocab Fun

Grades 2–6

This is a fun activity to get your students up and moving and learning new vocabulary words. Students will work in pairs to create a scene in which they are using a new vocabulary word throughout. Classmates will try to guess the definition of the word based on its usage and the context (important skills for any reader).

What You Need

- An open space to work
- Cards with vocabulary words

Student Learning Objective

Students will act and assume roles and interact in improvisations in effort to determine or clarify the meaning of unknown words and phrases

How to Do the Activity

1. Introduce or review the ideas of *"who, what, where"* improv (see Chapter 3).
2. Create a list of vocabulary words written on card stock (with the definition on the back) that are well suited for acting out.
3. Divide the class into pairs.
4. Ask each pair to take one card.
5. Explain that their job is to create a scene in which the given word would be vocalized three times. In the scene, the students must make clear the meaning of the word.
6. Allow 10–15 minutes for rehearsal
7. Students present scenes, and observers guess the meaning of the word based on the scene.

Example

Students are given the word "combine". Students decide they are going to play two scientists (the "who") who are doing an experiment. The "where" is a top-secret lab. The "what" is: what happens when they combine some pretty strange elements together. When the students play this scene out, they will vocalize the word a few times: "What happens if we combine this substance with that?" or "Oh no, did you combine the toxic chemical with soda pop?!" Then there is a big explosion and one student says: "Maybe we should have read the manual before we combined these two substances. OOPS!"

Standards Addressed

CCSS.ELA-LITERACY.L.3.4. Acquisition and Use: Determine or clarify the meaning of unknown and multiple-meaning words and phrases based on grade 3 reading and content, choosing flexibly from a range of strategies.

NCAS. Grade K-4 Theater Standard 2. Organize and develop artistic ideas and work. TH:Cr2.2. a. Collaborate with peers to devise meaningful dialogue in a guided drama experience.

"Run"—on–Sentence

Grades 2–6

In this fun and quick literacy game, students will work together to create a story. This is similar to the activity- add on story- where students add one word or phrase to collectively create a story. In this game, students will also physicalize the phrases- adding an idea and a motion- to help them recount the story being told.

What You Need

• An open space to work

Student Learning Objective

Students will use gestures and movement to collaboratively create or retell a story.

How to Play the Game

1. Ask students to make a circle allowing some wiggle room.
2. Explain to the students that they will create a story collectively with each student adding one phrase or sentence to the story.
3. With each phrase, ask the student to come up with a way to physicalize their phrase. This means that their body helps tell the story. For example, if they say: "I opened the door," they might move their hand forward miming opening a door.
4. Each student must repeat the phrase (and phrases) said before them as well as mimic the actions of the players that came before them. The last person must recount the entire story.

Helpful Hints

To help all students succeed in this activity, be strategic about where you place each of your students in the circle. A shy student would not be successful starting the game. Students who consistently demonstrate strong memory skills should be challenged and placed at the end of the circle. Students that may have more trouble recounting the story should be placed toward the start. You can have each player have one turn with the last student ending your story or you may go until the story comes to a natural close.

Standards Addressed

CCSS.ELA-Literacy.SL.3.4 Report on a topic or text, tell a story, or recount an experience with appropriate facts and relevant, descriptive details, speaking clearly at an understandable pace.

NCAS.Theater: Anchor Standard 1: Generate and conceptualize artistic ideas and work. TH:Cr1.1.1.c-Identify ways in which gestures and movement may be used to create or retell a story in guided drama experiences (e.g., process drama, story drama, creative drama).

References

Albers, P. (2006). Imagining the possibilities in multimodal curriculum design. *English Education*, 38(2), 75–101. https://www.jstor.org/stable/40173215

Brouillette, L. (2019). *Arts integration in diverse K-5 classrooms: Cultivating literacy skills and conceptual understanding.* Teachers College Press.

Brouillette, L., Childress-Evans, K., Hinga, B., & Farkas, G. (2014). Increasing engagement and oral language skills of ELLs through the arts in the primary grades. *Journal for Learning Through the Arts, 10*(1). https://escholarship.org/uc/item/8573z1fm

Cahnamann-Taylor, M., & McGovern, K. R. (2021). *Enlivening instruction with drama and improv: A guide for second language and world language teachers.* Routledge.

Calkins, L. (2020). *Teaching writing.* Heinemann.

Cazden, C., Cope, B., Kalantzis, M., Luke, A., Luke, C., & Nakata, M. (1996). A pedagogy of multiliteracies: Designing social futures. *Harvard Educational Review, 66*(1), 60–92.

Chisholm, J. S., & Whitmore, K. F. (2016). Bodies in space/bodies in motion/bodies in character: Adolescents bear witness to Anne Frank. *International Journal of Education & the Arts, 17*(5). http://www.ijea.org/v17n5/

Dayrell, E. (1990). *Why the sun and the moon live in the sky.* Clarion Books.

Donovan, L., & Pascale, L. (2012). *Integrating the arts across the curriculum.* Shell Education.

Fattal, L. R. (2019). Transmediational practices in a bilingual elementary classroom. *NABE Journal of Research and Practice*, *9*(2), 88–95. https://doi.org/10.1080/26390043.2019.1589295

Gilbert, A. G. (2002). *Teaching the three Rs through movement experiences*. National Dance Education Organization.

Goldberg, M. (2021). *Arts integration: Teaching subject matter through the arts in multicultural settings* (6th ed.). Routledge.

Greenfader, C. M., & Brouillette, L. (2014). Boosting language skills of ELLs through dramatization and movement. *The Reading Teacher*, *67*(3), 171–180.

Harste, J. C. (2014). Transmediation: What art affords our understanding of literacy. In 63rd *yearbook of the literacy research association* (pp. 88–102). Literacy Research Association.

Landay, E., & Wootton, K. (2012). *Linking literacy and the arts: A reason to read.*. Harvard Educational Press.

Mages, W. K. (2006). Drama and imagination: A cognitive theory of drama's effect on narrative comprehension and narrative production. *Research in Drama Education*, *11*(3), 329–340. https://doi.org/10.1080/13569780600900750

Palacio, R. J. (2012). *Wonder*. Alfred A Knopf.

Saldaña, J. (1995). *Drama of color: Improvisation with multiethnic folklore*. Heinemann.

Silverstein, S. (1981). *A light in the attic* (1st ed.). HarperCollins.

5 Moving Through History

Picture This...

It's Tuesday afternoon, and I'm working in an elementary school in Vermont. It's the third day in a row for indoor recess due to the below freezing wind chills. The students have not had much of a chance to move around during the day and let's just say they are a bit wiggly. I was working with a fifth-grade class in my role as a student teacher supervisor and had observed this group of students often over the course of the semester. I offered to work with the students during their social studies block that day because they needed something to get the kids up and moving and the classroom teacher knew about my background in theater. They were learning about Westward Expansion which is one of my favorite subjects to get moving with!

Earlier in the day, I observed this same group of students in math class. In the corner of the room, I noticed a young student who didn't seem very engaged. He rarely looked at the board or the teacher, and at one point the teacher walked over to take the pencil out of his hand because it was becoming a distraction. Later in the day, when I worked with this same group, he was hardly recognizable. I started the session by asking if they had ever seen a play, and his hand shot up in the air. The first slide on my PowerPoint was of *Hamilton* the Musical, and I posed the question about why plays and musicals were written. This student answered with gusto: "So, I have seen lots of plays. I love theater. I have seen *Hamilton* … and I get it. I get it. It's about History and you are working with us about histories and plays and stuff and" (and on he went). When it was time to act out their scenes about packing the wagon for travel on the Oregon Trail (see Figure 5.1), this student offered to go first. He stood front and center using his best "western" accent and performed his piece. "I can do lots of accents," he shared. He acted as the narrator for his group and with a booming voice and great expression, he narrated their scene about what they were packing in their covered wagon to prepare for their long journey on the Oregon Trail.

The student teacher came over after the session to share her amazement at this student's engagement in this activity: "I can't believe it. I have never seen that student so excited. He rarely listens when anyone is giving directions. In math class, he just draws on his paper constantly." I asked if any other students surprised her, and she said yes. Another student, who is often tired and quiet, also jumped in with gusto. "He is so capable," she affirms, "but he rarely shares his thoughts or speaks up in class." What shocked her most was that when it was his groups' time to share their scene, he had also taken on the role of the narrator, which meant he did the majority of the talking for the piece. The classroom teacher was also amazed by this students' efforts: "That made my day today, seeing this student acting and taking on leadership. Sometimes we let him sleep because he is always so tired and we know things at home are not great. That was

Figure 5.1 Students perform scenes based on their learning about Westward Expansion

probably the first time all year that he hasn't dozed off. And I've never heard him speak up like that."

This transformation of doodling and disengaged student to lead performer is not an anomaly. It's a common occurrence when students are engaged in lessons that integrate theater or movement into classroom instruction. Such activities bring out something in students that often goes under the radar. When students are offered alternative ways to engage with content, students step it up, and so many students surprise you. You see their untapped talents or interests. This increase in engagement results in deeper learning for these students and can impact their overall success at school. When students feel noticed and affirmed it often improves their performance in other subjects as well (Goldberg, 2021).

This lesson which asks students to create scenes based on their research about what folks packed to travel on the Oregon Trail is part of a unit I created called, *The Pioneer Musical*, which will be outlined more fully in this chapter. The goal is to create a musical with the class based on their learning about Westward Expansion that could be shared with others to help them learn about this historical period. Students learn songs from the period, dances, and create dramatic scenes based on their research. Having the goal of creating a musical that could be shared with other students focuses the work in a very important way. It requires students to take all they learned from their readings, organize it in a way to tell a story, making sure to include the most important information about this historical time period while making it interesting for their audience. Sound like an important skill to learn? In doing so, students are developing critical thinking and literacy skills for college and career readiness as identified by the Common Core State Standards such as "Determining the central ideas of a text, close reading to determine what the text says explicitly and to make logical inferences from it, and analyze how and why individuals, events or ideas develop and interact over the course of a text" (*Common Core State Standards, CCSS*). This approach also supports learning in history as identified by *The C3 Framework for Social Studies State Standards* (*C3*) created by the National Council for the Social Studies (2013) as it encourages students to conduct historical inquiry which "involves acquiring knowledge about significant events, developments, individuals, groups, documents, places and ideas to support investigations about the past. Acquiring relevant knowledge requires assembling information from a wide variety of sources in an integrative process" (*C3*, p. 45).

Creating scenes based on students' learning about a historical period has other benefits for students. It engages emotions in learning, teaches empathy, and provides opportunities for students to collaborate with their peers. This chapter will share some ways in which theater and movement can be integrated into your social studies curriculum to increase engagement, deepen learning, and teach valuable lessons that are integral to understanding social studies content to prepare for college, career, and civic life. It is one of the subjects that is a natural fit for arts integration for a variety of reasons that will be covered in this chapter.

Packing the Wagon: How Do We Make History Real and Relevant for Students?

One of the reasons why integrating theater with social studies is impactful is that it can make historical events more real and relevant for students. Take the "pack the wagon" activity discussed in the opening story. In this activity, students are put into groups and given a short excerpt to read about one aspect of life on the Oregon Trail. Topics include the Homestead Act, about The Oregon Trail, challenges traveling on the trail, interactions with Native Americans, and packing the wagon. Students are tasked with reading the excerpt, deciding about the most important details to include, and putting this information into a short skit.

When students work on the "pack your wagon" scene, they read about all the items that pioneers had to pack as well as how to prepare the wagon for travel. When students share their work for the first time, it is often on a very surface level. They might choose to have the scene be about a family and they often act out filling the wagon with various items identified in the reading. When students share their work, they are pushed to dig deeper by asking questions such as:

- "What did you have to leave behind to make room for all those supplies?"
- "What would it be like to pack only part of what you own because most of it wouldn't fit?"
- "If you had to move to California tomorrow only taking what you could fit in your minivan, what would you have to let go of?"
- "Are your friends and family coming with you?"
- "How will it feel to have to leave some of the people you love behind?"

Such questions bring these abstract ideas like Westward Expansion into a framework that students can relate to. Having to put it into a skit where they play it out helps them connect to the material in a very real way. When students rehearse the scenes again, they are often much more emotionally charged. Students might portray children who beg to bring their teddy bear or favorite toys or ask parents questions like, "Why can't grandma come with us?" Bringing these ideas closer to home can help students make a personal connection to events in history which makes it more real and relevant. It also taps into their emotions which increases their retention of the information. Hardiman (2012) has shown that when students engage their emotions in the learning process, it fires a different part of the brain that connects to long-term memory, and therefore it increases retention. This process of creating skits based on a historical event also allows students to access the material from a place of curiosity. While there are readings and themes assigned to them, they can focus on the aspects of the content that most interest them, which helps with motivation and engagement.

C3 Skill Building Using the Arts: Learning Skills that Prepare Students to Be Active Citizens in a Healthy Democracy

Using theater and movement to embody historical figures or creating plays about historical time periods not only supports the learning of social studies content, but it teaches students valuable skills that prepare them for civic engagement which is an identified goal of most social studies curriculum. Skills such as active listening, empathy, understanding perspectives, and collaboration are vital to ensuring a healthy democracy where citizens can discuss, debate, and work together to address the needs of society. *The C3 Framework for Social Studies State Standards* (C3) was written to support schools in achieving these goals in their social studies curriculum and suggest that the arts are an effective avenue for doing so, "Children and adolescents are naturally curious about the complex and multifaceted world they inhabit. But they quickly become disengaged when instruction is limited to reading textbooks to answer end-of-chapter questions and taking multiple-choice tests that may measure content knowledge but do little to measure how knowledge is meaningful and applicable in the real world" (*C3*). Arts engagement provides opportunities to achieve C3 goals such as developing empathy, perspective taking, active listening, and collaboration skills, each explored in more depth in the next section.

Teaching Empathy

Using theater as a tool to engage with social studies content can help students learn and practice empathy. The "pack the wagon" activity exemplifies this outcome. In effort to portray these characters on stage, students had to imagine what it was like to be a person living in that time period making tough decisions and attempt to feel what it must have been like to do so. As students performed other scenes from *The Pioneer Musical*, they had to "walk in the shoes" of those who walked the Oregon Trail or (so they learned) in some cases have no shoes at all due to the extensive walking that often destroyed footwear mid-journey (see Box 5.1 for more ways to "walk in the shoes" of historical figures).

Empathy or the ability to feel and understand others' feelings and needs is not only essential to learning social studies, but is vital to student success on many levels (Borba, 2018). Borba (2018) in her extensive research on

History Walk: Walking in the Shoes of Historical Figures or through Historical Events

Encourage students' empathy by doing a history walk. This activity is built on Viola Spolin's *spacewalk* (1963). Ask students to walk around the room and prepare to enact what you call out. Start with easy directions like walk quickly, slowly, hop on one foot. Then move on to engaging the imagination: walk like going through peanut butter or splashing in puddles. The water might turn quickly to ice, and they can skate on the imaginary pond. Use this tool to experience social studies content: walk as if traveling on the Oregon Trail and show how tired you are walking 15 miles today. You can connect to marches for social justice or to experience what many children have to do to walk for water in various countries where fresh water must be collected miles away from homes.

Box 5.1 Outlines *History Walk,* an Activity for Using Walking and Theater to "Walk in the Shoes" of People in History

the impact of technology on social skills such as empathy maintains that "empathy is at the core of everything that makes a school caring, a teacher responsive, and a society civilized. When empathy wanes, narcissism, distrust, aggression, bullying, and hate rise- and schools suffer" (p. 22). She argues that we must actively teach empathy in schools and that doing so is essential to creating a safe, caring, and inclusive learning climate that directly impacts students' learning and academic success. When students are empathetic, they are less aggressive, better communicators, more resilient, more engaged, and score higher academically (Borba, 2018).

Utilizing the arts, especially theater, in the learning process can help to develop students' empathy (Goldberg, 2021). Foundational to becoming empathetic is being able to recognize and identify emotions (Borba, 2018). Theater work is grounded in this ability. In effort to portray a character and what that character is feeling, actors need to get in touch with their own emotions. In effort to portray an emotion, you must be able to identify it, recognize it, and name it. When portraying sadness or happiness, actors often think about a time when they felt these emotions and that in turn helps their face and body represent it similarly.

Using Theater to Practice Empathy as Communication

Izhak Berkovich (2020) conducted a large-scale search of all the empirical studies on empathy and K-12 teaching to investigate how "empathy" was being understood in an educational context. One defining element is the notion of empathy as communication (a way of interacting with each other that includes a combination of verbal and non-verbal responsiveness to others' emotions that embodies levels of sympathy.) Engaging theater techniques in the teaching process effectively attends to this last goal because communication using verbal and non-verbal cues is central to the art of acting. This theme has been covered extensively throughout this book (see Chapter 3, "Theater Basics" and "Improvisation 101" and Chapter 4, "Reader as actor").

Lessons to Practice Empathy as Communication

Improvisation: Acting Out Scenarios (Chapter 3)
Brown Bag Improv (Chapter 3)

Teaching the Skill of Understanding Varying Perspectives

Perspective taking is one of the core competencies identified by Borba (2018) and considered what she calls the "cognitive side to empathy" (p. 25) because it forces you to recognize the emotions or feelings of others, and make sense of it, answering the question: "why might this person feel this way?" Borba argues that teaching this skill is essential for educating our students, but also for "educating for humanity" (p. 25). Learning to see issues from another perspective is essential for students to understand the complexity of a situation and for deeper understanding of, for example, literature (how various characters see an event) or history (the various sides to a particular issue) and be a part of a learning community (where they can understand how other students may feel about or see a particular situation), to future citizens who can see various perspectives on an issue facing society. Theater is an excellent way to teach and practice the skill of perspective taking. To portray another person, one must try to see the world through their eyes and emulate that world view on stage. Borba shares an idea from a lesson on *Romeo and Juliet* where a teacher puts paper feet on the floor to represent different characters in the story and asks students to literally stand in another person's shoes in effort to vocalize the happenings in the play from that character's perspective.

Understanding perspective is a core principle of the C3 Framework. It acknowledges that history is interpretive and that there are multiple perspectives on historical events because people construct their understanding of an event through their lens which is shaped by their beliefs, ideas, and experiences. Teaching students to seek out these multiple perspectives through various sources is essential to them answering questions about key events in history. The C3 Framework suggests that students use perspective to compare past to present: "It also requires recognizing that perspectives change over time, so that historical understanding requires developing a sense of empathy with people in the past whose perspectives might be very different from those of today" (p. 47). Teaching history with a focus on perspective also helps our students understand that much of our history has been told through one lens: often Eurocentric and from a person who is white. Considering various perspectives helps students to see who are the dominant voices in history and what voices are left out (Goldberg, 2021).

Lesson plans for practicing empathy and perspective taking (both included at the end of this chapter):

> *Storytelling/perspective taking*
> *Writing monologues*

Embodying Democracy

One of the main justifications for social studies content in schools is to prepare students to enter civic life and be part of a just and civil society that can respectfully listen, disagree, and engage in collective decision making. This takes citizens who can listen deeply, have empathy, see various perspectives, and ultimately collaborate with all people to support the common good. These skills are essential to theater making which makes it an ideal tool in the classroom as it provides opportunities for students to practice such skills.

Active Listening for Understanding

The skill of listening is in my opinion highly under emphasized in schools and the curriculum. It is essential for many of the skills that have been discussed such as empathy and understanding perspectives. It is also necessary for civic engagement. As the C3 standards acknowledge "civil and democratic discourse within a diverse, collaborative context [is] both a purpose and outcome of a strong meaningful, and substantive social studies education" (p. 21). Democratic discourse requires active listening, taking the time to listen to each other in effort to understand their perspective. This skill is also acknowledged in the Common Core as an anchor standard for speaking and listening: "participate effectively in a range of conversations and collaborations with diverse partners, build on other's ideas and express their own clearly and persuasively" (*CCSS*, p. 22).

What is active listening? It's the kind of listening that goes beyond hearing what another person says and seeks to process what is heard in a way that creates deeper understanding. Active listening often results in a response: either another question, affirmation, or acknowledgment of what the other person has shared, but not always agreement (Knight, 2015). This skill is not often explicitly taught in schools and yet is key to learning and being part of a community of learners. Theater improvisation is an excellent way to teach listening skills, as you must be very present to accomplish the task. You can't be thinking about something else while you are improvising. You must be focused on what your partner says, so you can respond in the moment. See Chapter 3 "Improvisation 101" for explicit ways in which improv can be taught and used to teach listening.

Collaboration

At the end of my arts integration course for preservice teachers, students are asked to make a vlog about their key learnings from the course. One aspect of learning that is frequently shared is that the use of theater gives them extensive practice in collaboration. Most of the activities presented in this book depend on collaboration skills: students are put into groups to create sculptures that bring a poem to life, work in teams to demonstrate how penguins move to stay warm, or to create skits based on their learning in social studies. The "pack your wagon" activity demonstrates how theater requires collaboration. The need for collaboration skills has become even more vital considering our current political climate that has become so divisive. Collaboration skills are also more necessary for work, as most business models are organized in teams. Yet, it isn't often explicitly taught in schools. Working in groups to create theater and dance pieces supports learning in this area, offering students a way to practice what can be challenging skills. Students have to take and share ideas, listen deeply, and share leadership. When teaching collaboration in your classroom, start small. Begin having students work in pairs, then build up to groups of three. Maybe have students work in groups of four and five by the end of the year. Revisit Chapter 2, "Learning how to collaborate" for more ways to teach this valuable skill in your classroom.

Activities to Practice Collaboration

> *Diamonds* (Chapter 2)
> *Rock Passing Game from Ghana* (Chapter 2)

Establishing a Where (Chapter 3)
Sculptures (Chapter 3)

Playbuilding and Creating *The Pioneer Musical*: Integrating Theater and Movement with Westward Expansion Content

The *Pioneer Musical* was created using a structure called "playbuilding" (Tarlington & Michaels, 1995), which is an excellent way to engage in social studies content using theater and movement. Playbuilding, simply put, means to build a play, but collectively with a group of people. This process focuses on creating theme plays, which means they are not centered on a character or their journey, but based on students' reactions, thoughts, and explorations on a theme. This process is well suited to creating plays with students about historical events, as you can choose a theme like the American Revolution, Westward Expansion, the Civil Rights Movement, or Women in History. Each of the scenes created can be one aspect or event that aligns with that theme. The dialogue is created through improvisation (making up the scenes on the spot) instead of script writing. This is particularly effective for a few reasons. First, writing a script with a group is challenging, so having small groups use improvisation to create the script works more effectively. Second, the process is what is most important. When students use a script, there is some learning that occurs, but the benefits are so much greater when students have to enact the creative process: they read the content, decide what is most important to share, make decisions about who, what, where, and how to tell their story. This process forces them to think critically and collaborate, and in doing so, deepens their learning.

In effort to create *The Pioneer Musical*, students engage in a few different processes to create the "content" and then all these pieces are combined for a final piece. These parts can be used independently in your classroom to enliven and enrich your social studies lessons, or they can be used to build a play. Each of the activities will be described briefly here, using *The Pioneer Musical* as an example, with individual lesson plans provided at the end of the chapter. Now have your students "circle the wagons" (see Box 5.2) and get moving:

Box 5.2 Using the Idea of "Circle the Wagons" to Bring Students to the Rug for Learning

- **Learning songs and dances**: Learning songs and dance from the historical period you are studying is an excellent way to engage in learning. Westward Expansion is a rich source for music as many of our traditional American tunes come from this time period (*Home on the Range, Buffalo Gals, Old Dan Tucker, Oh Suzanna*). Teach students songs like *Wait for the Wagon* that can be used as your opening number (see Figure 5.2) or *Home on the Range* to end it. You can also teach square dance (see Box 5.3, *Dance and Pioneer Life: The Hoedown*) that can be performed in your *Pioneer Musical*. Teaching dances that align with historical periods is an excellent way to engage movement in learning and students will respond favorably! There are so many videos and resources that can be found online to support your efforts to integrate dance with any time period or area of study.
- The **chores warm up** is a movement activity where students share their learning about what children did daily in this time period and while traveling on the trail. It can be used as a daily movement break or as the opening scene of your musical. This concept can be adapted to integrate movement into any social studies unit. (See lesson plan:

Figure 5.2 Students practice the opening number for *The Pioneer Musical*. They sing *Wait for the* Wagon as they cross the stage with their "covered wagon"

(Photograph shared with permission from IAA)

Warming up to History: "Chores" at the end of this chapter for directions for leading this activity.)

- **One liners** (Tarlington & Michaels, 1995) can be created by students to summarize their main take aways about a content area. Students respond to prompts such as "When I think of Pioneers, I think of ...." These are used as a frame for your musical, introducing each of the scenes that students create, and can be adapted to any theme. (One-liners are included in the process articulated in *Scene building for Historical Plays or* Musicals lesson plan at the end of the chapter).

- Creating **monologues** (see full lesson plan at the end of the chapter) is another way to build content for a script. For *The Pioneer Musical*, students can either write a monologue about a historical figure from the time period, a fictitious person traveling on the trail (based on their research), or they can write journal entries or letters home recounting their experiences on the trail. Choosing a few of the monologues or journal entries to be read/performed intermittently can help to create a rich and entertaining performance and allow a few students to shine

The Hoedown

This dance from the early 1800s was named the hoedown because folks were supposed to put the hoe (from farming) down and join their community in some fun. Teach this dance to share with students how folks in the past socialized.

Steps

Have students form two lines facing a partner and do the following moves. (Note: Most moves should take a whole count of 8).

> **Clap to the beat**: Start by encouraging students to clap along to the beat- feeling the strong beat of 4.
>
> **Bow to your partner**: Students can bow or curtsy to their partner.
>
> **Greet your partner**: Students take three steps forward toward their partner (with a touch of their foot down on the count of four). Then take three steps back (and touch).
>
> **Do-si-do:** Students step toward their partner, then rotate around each other, always keeping their eyes forward. Each student moves clockwise.
>
> **Swing your Partner**: Students walk toward their partner, link arms, and skip in a circular motion (then switch arms and go in the other direction).
>
> **Promenade:** Each pair links arms and moves through the middle of the two lines.

Now lead the call. The key to doing this dance successfully in your classroom is if you do the calling. This means that you call each move (which means students must be on their toes). Work to find a rhythm with the calls so that students can start the moves on the count of one of each set of beats.

> Suggested songs: Buffalo Gals, Turkey in the Straw

Box 5.3 Dance & Pioneer Life: Teaching the Hoedown

(see Figure 5.3). This structure can be adapted to create content for a play from any time period.

- **Scene building** creates the bulk of the content for your musical, with students working in groups to create scenes based on their own research. Students are put into groups, given a reading about a certain aspect of your study, and create scenes. If you need more structure for scene building, try the lesson ***Talking Tableaux.***

The Pioneer Musical: Example of a script format

Once you have completed all the lessons in this unit, taught songs and dance, and created scenes based on readings, put it all together to create a performance to share with your school community. This is a possible order for your performance. Don't forget to add music in between scenes to help with transitions.

Wait for the Wagon song & musical number

Chores scene

Scene 1: Pack the Wagon (introduced by a one liner)

Figure 5.3 Warren Ouellette performs a monologue in a performance in a *The History Play*
(Photo granted with permission from student)

Journal entry 1

Scene 2: The Homestead Act (introduced by a one liner)

Scene 3: About the Oregon Trail (introduced by a one liner)

Journal entry 2

Scene 3: A day in the life of a pioneer (introduced by a one liner)

Journal entry 3

Scene 4: Challenges on the trail (introduced by a one liner)

Hoedown dance

Scene 5: Relations with Native Americans (introduced by a one liner)

Journal entry 4

Scene 6: Circle the Wagons: ending another day on the trail (introduced by a one liner)

Song: *Home on the Range*

LESSON PLANS THAT INTEGRATE DANCE AND THEATER WITH SOCIAL STUDIES

 ## Writing Monologues

Grades 3–6

A monologue is a great way to integrate theater into a social studies or literacy lesson and for students to dig deeper into characterization. A monologue is a first-person account of a story that helps us understand more about who they are or how they see the world or an event. Students can research a person in history, a character in a book, or write their own about their life.

What You Need

- Character sketch graphic organizer
- Content for research (on-line curated resources or books)

Student Learning Objective

Students will write a monologue based on their research of a historical figure or character from a work of fiction, identifying relevant details and key events from their life which they will perform in some capacity for their classmates.

How to Do the Activity

The format is provided here, the specifics of each step are provided at the end of the lesson plan.

1. Try the process of creating a monologue first with a well-known fairytale (*Jack in the Beanstalk, Cinderella, 3 Little Pigs,* etc.).
2. Ask students to choose one character from a fairytale and answer the questions identified in the **Character Sketch**.
3. Ask students to use answers from the character sketch and combine to write a **monologue** (about one paragraph) written in first person narrative.
4. Have students **perform their monologue**. (They can read their monologue or perform without the script using improvisation techniques.)
5. In the next lesson, ask students to choose from a list of historical figures (based on the curriculum you are studying) and repeat the process. (This time including some time for research and or reading of provided materials.)

Helpful Hint: Important Reminder: Respectful Representation

When students are embodying other people, it is imperative that you lay the groundwork first about respectful representation, meaning that it is vital that students do not use stereotypes of any kind to mimic someone from another gender, race, or cultural background. One way this can be avoided entirely (albeit important to discuss) is to use what Stanislavski called the "magic if." This means that when actors take on a role they do it in a way that "if" they magically were that person, how would they act in the given situation. Therefore, the tools for the storytelling are your own body and voice and you are simply telling this story as if it happened to you. If there are concerns that a student was choosing a historical figure that was much different from their own cultural, racial, or gender background, you can *change the perspective* of the piece (see "Changing Perspectives" under Extensions to see how this could work.)

Reflection and Wrap Up

- Were there some common themes that you noticed across all the performances? What might this tell us about important historical figures or change agents?
- Did the act of embodying these characters (either your experience of performing or observing) bring these characters more to life for you? Why or why not?

Extensions/Adaptations

Changing perspective: Try this activity, but change the perspective encouraging students to tell the key story in the monologue from another person's point of view. For example, when using this process in a unit on the underground railroad, students were asked to change the perspective for the monologue. For example, students researched stories about real people who either traveled on the underground railroad or helped others along the route. Then they were asked to change the perspective, and tell the story from the point of view of a young person who witnessed this event. Example: Students read about a man who sent himself to freedom. They completed the process, and then, took on the role of a child in the wagon who was carrying this package to the post office. They were able to recount many of the same details, but telling the story through their lens provided an opportunity to have their representation more fitting for their own identity.

Steps for creating and performing a monologue

Step 1**: Create a Character Sketch**

Chosen character (historical figure or character from a book): _____

What do you know about this character based on the text or your research?

They come from or live? _____

They are how old? _____

They love to? _____

Fun fact about your character? (or what about them makes them unique):

_____

Share a story about a pivotal event in their life that taught them a life lesson or changed the course of their life:

_____

How did this event affect the direction of their life or those around them? Explain any lessons learned from this event:

_____

Step 2: **Write Your Monologue**

Now, pretend you are this character, and write a short monologue (brief story and first-person perspective that tells about who you are and what you experienced) using these key details from your character sketch.

Helpful hint: A monologue is like a short story. It has a beginning, middle, and end. And often includes a moral or lesson learned.

Step 3: **Perform Your Monologue**

Much of the fun (and learning) comes from students performing their monologues and having their classmates figure out who is being portrayed. Students may read the monologue, but encourage them to try to improvise instead by simply using the format of introducing themselves and sharing their story. This makes the sharing much more dramatic and engaging for your audience.

Extensions/Adaptations

Studying Change Agents: This can be a great way to have students research change agents throughout history. Have students choose an important figure who has impacted the world or the lives of others and complete this process.

Standards Addressed

C3 Framework. D2.His.3.3-5. Generate questions about individuals and groups who have shaped significant historical changes and continuities.

CCSSELA-Literacy.W.3.Write narratives to develop real or imagined experiences or events using effective technique, descriptive details, and clear event sequences. (a) Establish a situation and introduce a narrator and/or characters; organize an event sequence that unfolds naturally. (b) Use dialogue and descriptions of actions, thoughts, and feelings to develop experiences and events.

NCAS. TH:Cr1.1.3.a. Create roles, imagined worlds, and improvised stories in a drama/theatre work.

Talking Tableaux

Grade K-6

A tableaux is a great way to begin integrating drama and movement into your history lessons. After choosing a moment in history to explore, students create a tableaux or frozen "picture" of the event by thinking about who they might be in the scene. When you tap them on the shoulder, they must say something. They can express something they are "seeing or hearing" in the scene or how they are feeling about what is happening. Using tableaux is a simple way to begin to dramatize historical events encouraging all students to engage in the material as if they were there.

What You Need

- An account of a historical event, a picture, or story of an event to share
- An open space
- A person who acts as documenter (if you so choose)

Student Learning Objective

With prompting and support, students identify characters and setting and create dialogue to embody a story in guided drama.

How to Do the Activity

1. Any historical event or series of events can be the source for this activity. It is best to choose an event that either has a large number of characters or represents a weighted event where there are many varied feelings about what is occurring. Examples: the Boston Tea Party (or a few key events that led up to the American Revolution), the landing on Plymouth Rock and the creation of the Mayflower Compact, the speech given by Samuel Adams to a group of British soldiers, patriots, and sympathizers.
2. Read an excerpt about the chosen historical event.
3. Ask students to think about a person who might be in this scene.

4. Create a tableaux. Ask one student to go on stage and make a pose of a person that might be in this scene. Ask the next student to add to that pose by either relating to the person on stage, or thinking about another person who might be in this scene. Keep adding until as many students who chose to are in the tableaux.

5. Set the stage for this historical event by asking some key questions about what they "see" or might "feel" about what is happening in this event. For example, staging the landing on Plymouth Rock landing, you might ask: "what would it feel like to land in a new place, and be cold and wet and tired, and not have any real plan for what to do once you got there?" Reading about this event, it seems as if there were no laws. Ask students: "Should they follow King George's laws, lacking any of their own, or should they create new ones?"

6. One at a time, tap each student on the shoulder, and ask them to say what they might say in this situation.

7. Students may simply state how they feel, or they may respond to what was said before them, such as "I'm cold," "How will we get shelter here?" and "Who's in charge anyway?". If they are on opposite sides of the political divide, for example, if you were recreating the speech by Samuel Adams, ask what they would say if they were playing a patriot and other students what they might say if they are playing a loyalist.

Helpful Hints

This is a great way to begin building a scene based on an historical event. By taking the time to tap each student one at a time, you are ensuring that each child speaks and that they listen to and respond to what is said before them.

- If this will be used to create a scene in your play, consider recording or documenting lines said so they can be turned in to a scene for a future performance.
- If you are studying a chain of events, you can create a tableaux for each event and then perform them in sequence like a living time line. It can be helpful to add a narrator who gives a short introduction for each tableaux. This is a great way to address another C3 standard (C3. D2.His.1.3-5. Create and use a chronological sequence of related events to compare developments that happened at the same time.)

Reflect and Wrap Up

- Discuss why there were varying views about each of these historical events.
- If doing a sequence of events, ask students to share if perspectives changed over time. If students did not change their perspectives in the scene work, ask if they should, why or why not?
- Consider staging the sequence of tableaus again having them consider how their feelings might change through the course of these events (might their feelings get stronger, lessen, or change over time).

Extension/Adaptation

Using primary sources: It is great to find primary sources to add to these dramatizations. For example, if studying the landing on Plymouth Rock and the introduction of the Mayflower compact, consider having a student read part of the original document as part of your dramatization. For example, the scene could end with this reading, with each student (character) one at a time agreeing to sign and saying "aye." Using small sections of primary source materials can deepen and enrich the theatrical and educational experience.

For younger students, simplify the process and use a theme as the source for the tableaux. For example, in a study on community, ask each student to become a community helper and make a pose to embody that character. As you tap on their shoulders, they can say who they are and what they do to help their community.

Connect to literacy: This activity can easily be adapted into a literacy lesson. Make a tableaux from one page of a picture book with multiple characters. What might each of them say about what is happening? String multiple tableaux together to perform the sequence of events in the story.

Standards Addressed

C3.D2. His.4.3-5. Explain why individuals and groups during the same historical period differed in their perspectives.

NCAS. TH.Pr4.1 k a. With prompting and support, identify characters and setting in dramatic play or a guided drama experience

NCAS. Pr4.1 3 a. Modify the dialog and action to change the story in a drama/theatre work.

Warming Up to History: "Chores"

Grade K-5

This activity requires students to collect information about what people did in historical time periods and create a movement to embodied it. The example given is about Westward Expansion, but can be adapted to any content. In this lesson, students create a movement for "chores" children had to do. This can be done in one lesson or built over the course of a unit. Add music and use it as a daily warm-up or as the opening scene of your play.

What You Need

- Read-aloud, selection of readings, or some way to present content
- Music
- Board or chart paper

Student Learning Objective

Students will create movements that express an idea (gained from research and/or learning about a historical time period), and in doing so compare life in specific historical time periods to life today.

How to Do the Activity

1. Identify some type of source that will be used to present content—a read aloud, provided text, etc.
2. Ask students to pay close attention to action (what the people did in these historical contexts).
3. Generate a list.
4. One by one, go down the list, and ask all the students to move as if doing that "chore" or activity.
5. After children act out each chore, choose one movement from all you see to be the "move" for this action (that the whole class will do).
6. Build a sequence that encourages students to perform all the movements in a series.
7. Add music.
8. Perform this daily as morning "chores" or warm-up.

9. Throughout the process, use this activity as an opportunity to talk about things that are different from what folks did in this historical period to today. (Or in the case of community helpers, how action-oriented their work is.)

Reflect and Wrap Up

• What do students notice about the kinds of things folks had to do in this time period (or in this role)? How does it compare to their life experience?

Extensions/Adaptations

For younger students: You may decide to skip the research and instead have a list ready to go. Ask all students to move as if doing the chore or work. It may be better to allow all students to do the action they choose, rather than agreeing on a common movement for all.

Create a scene: This series of actions can be used to create a theatrical scene. Ask a student to introduce the scene with a one-liner such as "being a pioneer kid was hard, we had a lot of chores to do!" or "Community helpers do so much to help us in our community. They (fill in the blank)." Ask each student to, in turn, introduce their "move" and do the action, or have one student introduce the "move" and all students do the action.

Connect to Other Subjects

Literacy: Create a set of movements that depict the journey of a character. What actions do they do to move throughout the story? (For example, Goldilocks walks to house, collects flowers, enters house, tests out porridge, sits in chairs and beds, runs home).

Science: This works well as an astronaut warm up—all the actions they need to do to prepare for space travel (dress for space, helmet on, check controls, simulate flight, etc.) or create a series of moves to depict a life cycle of a plant or animal.

Standards Addressed

C3.D2. His.2.3-5. Compare life in specific historical time periods to life today.

NCAS. DA:Cr2.1.2 b. Choose movements that express an idea or emotion, or follow a musical phrase.

Diamonds and The Civil Rights Movement

Grades 3–6

This activity is built off the **diamonds** activity introduced in Chapter 2. In this activity, students enter the classroom to find a slew of photographs from the Civil Rights Movement in the 1960s. They are tasked with viewing photos and choosing one that "speaks to them" and then creating three movements to depict either the actions in the photographs or the emotions it generates in either the people in the photograph or the student. Movements will be combined in the diamonds' activity and performed.

What You Need

- Open space
- Music from the 1960s—freedom songs
- Photographs from the 1960s Civil Rights Movement

Student Learning Objective

Students will explore and create movements inspired by photographs from the Civil Rights Movement and both generate questions about and offer thoughts on how individuals and groups have impacted historical change.

How to Do the Activity

Start with the activity **diamonds** (see lesson plan Chapter 2).
Adding historical context:

1. Once students have practiced the activity of *diamonds*, it's time to add some content.
2. Provide photographs depicting events in the Civil Rights Movement of the 1960s. (Have these scattered around the floor when students enter the classroom.)
3. Ask students to walk around the room taking some time to view most of the photographs. Have music from the period playing such as: Lift Every Voice, This Little Light of Mine, Wade in the Water, We Shall Overcome.
4. Remind students that this is a silent activity.
5. After about 5 minutes, ask students to walk toward a picture that sparks their curiosity.

6. Ask each student to choose one photograph.

7. Ask students to create three moves that either are seen in the photograph or depict emotions emulated in the photograph (or even a movement that encapsulates their emotional response to the photograph).

8. Once students have three moves, ask them to get into a groups of four and use these moves in the diamonds activity.

9. Explain to the students that they are now taking these moves and thinking like choreographers. Therefore, they can repeat the moves multiple times or they can expand upon the movement—making it bigger or smaller, or exploring the movement more fully. (Try sidecoaching by asking: "Where does this move want to go next?")

10. Ask students to name one common movement they noticed in many of the photographs? (Marching, fists in the air, holding signs, etc.). Tell students to march when they don't have an idea or at the end when they are waiting for other groups to finish.

11. Ask for voices off and have students lead and follow for a few rounds.

12. Break the group into half-half perform and half observe.

13. Discuss.

Reflection and Wrap Up

• How did it make you feel to perform/view these movements?

• What did you notice while watching your classmates perform their moves? Were there common movements? What does this tell us about what was happening at this point in history?

• How did connecting to emotions affect your understanding or engagement with these photographs or time period?

• The Civil Rights Movement is ongoing. Can you think of issues today that might be worth protesting or marching for?

Standards Addressed

C3. D2.His.3.3-5. Generate questions about individuals and groups who have shaped significant historical changes and continuities.

NCAS.DA:Cr1.1.2a. Explore movement inspired by a variety of stimuli (e.g., music/sound, text, objects, images, symbols, observed dance, and experiences) and suggest additional sources for movement ideas.

Scene Building for Historical Plays or Musicals

Grades 3–6

Students become experts in one area of a chosen historical event or time period and stage a dramatic scene based on their learning. After reading a section of an informational text, students work in groups to create a scene to share the key ideas in the reading and bring the content to life through characters, setting, and action.

What You Need

- Open space in your classroom
- Selected readings for groups

Student Learning Objective

Students will work in groups to create a dramatic representation using improvisation based on their close reading of an information text. They will determine the main idea of the text, recount key details, and make decisions about the most salient information to share in their piece.

How to Do the Activity

1. Prepare reading selections depending on the number of students in your classroom. Readings should provide various events or perspectives about a key historical event. For example: Westward Expansion (packing the wagon, the Homestead Act, About the Oregon Trail, relations with Native Americans, and Challenges on the trail).
2. Put students in groups of 3 or 4.
3. Students read the selection (either as a group or individually) and agree on the key facts that should be shared in their scene
4. Students agree on *who, what, and where* (see "Improvisation 101" Chapter 3).
5. If students are having a hard time getting started, suggest they start by creating a tableaux (see *Talking Tableaux*).
6. Students share their scenes with the class. Classmates offer one affirmation and one challenge.

7. Facilitate more feedback as needed, by asking questions such as: "What was the main idea of this scene?" "Who are the characters in this scene and what do they want?" "Was it clear what the (insert concept like Homestead Act) was?" This offers further guidance for the process as students must be reminded that the point of a play is to communicate with the audience. If some things are not clear, it's time to rework and revise.

8. Students go back for a second rehearsal to make any necessary changes to improve their presentation of the content.

9. Students create a *one liner*- that can be used to introduce their scene (or you can have all students create a one-liner about the content area.) You can offer a sentence starter like: "Being a pioneer was hard, we had to." Choose a handful of the created one-liners to introduce your scenes.

10. Perform: Plan to have students perform for other classes or the school community.

Reflect and Wrap Up

- Your questions at the end of this activity will depend on the content. If you are for example having a group of scenes about events leading up to the American Revolution, the question might be something like: "What were some of the common emotions and or sentiments presented in these scenes? How do you think that may have impacted how and why we finally decided to go to war with England? Or if its scenes about Westward Expansion, you might ask something like: "What were some of the challenges of traveling out West? Benefits? Do you think it was worth it in the end to make this trek?" Overall, the idea is to have them consider these parts in effort to understand some-thing about the whole; help students to understand how these various events help us either see multiple perspectives of a historical event or give a more complete picture of this time period.

Extensions/Adaptations

For younger students: In effort to engage younger students in dramatiza-tion, you can take the role of the narrator and have students work as a class to act out what is being said. Instead of students being put into groups and doing readings on their own, you can do a read aloud about a historical period, event, or concept.

Standards Addressed

NCAS. TH:Cr1.1.3.a. Create roles, imagined worlds, and improvised stories in a drama/theatre work.

CCSS.ELA-LITERACY.RI.3.2 Determine the main idea of a text; recount the key details and explain how they support the main idea.

CCSS.ELA-LITERACY.SL.3.4 Report on a topic or text, tell a story, or recount an experience with appropriate facts and relevant, descriptive details, speaking clearly at an understandable pace.

Compass Rose and Moving Maps

Grades 2–6

In this lesson, students will learn about a Compass Rose and what it is used for. They will practice following directions: NSEW by using direction cards while moving on an imaginary map of the United States.

What You Need

- Large space to work, it can be helpful to use the school gym for this activity
- A visual of a Compass Rose & United States map
- Direction cards: with 3 directions on each card (walk 5 steps N, walk 10 steps S, walk 3 steps W, where do you land?) and the end location on the back.
- Music

Student Learning Objective

Students will explore movement inspired by maps and a Compass Rose to explore basic tenants of map construction.

How to Do the Activity

1. Create cards prior to this lesson. (Note: Because the map on the floor is imaginary and all students' feet are different sizes which means they will take different size steps, the end location may not be exact. But that is ok, and it allows for a great conversation at the end of the game about how maps were created- how it was necessary to make some kind of scale to ensure accuracy, etc.)

2. Begin the lesson by sharing a picture of a Compass Rose (explain its use, creation, purpose, and possibly its history.)

3. Ask students to stand and raise their arms in the air. As you call out directions such as North, South, East, and West, students move their arms in that direction. This can mimic a Simon Says game: "Compass Rose says north," "Compass rose says "south," "now West". "I didn't say Compass Rose!")

4. Next display a map of the United States

5. Ask students to imagine a map of the US on the floor. Ask for a volunteer to go onto the "map" on the floor. Ask students to move around the space. When you say stop, ask the class: "approximately where is student X on the map?" (Florida, Vermont, Kansas, etc.). If it's too tricky to name states, you can do regions like, you are in the North West or South West.

6. Next, give 8–10 students a card. Ask them to go onto the stage area. Play music, and ask them all to follow their directions and move on the map as directed. (Ask them not to look at the back of the card.) Once all players have gotten to their final spot, stop the music, and ask for volunteers from the audience to guess where they landed. For example, an observer may say, "I think Kelly landed in Georgia," and then Kelly would look at the card to see if they were close. If they make it to the same location, great, if not, have students look at the map displayed to discuss: "were you close?" "You were supposed to be in North Carolina, but you can see on the map you were close." Or you can have students give a thumbs up if they were close.

7. Switch players so all students can have a chance to move on the map.

8. Discuss and reflect

Reflect and Wrap UP

• Ask students what is a Compass Rose is and how it relates to maps.

• Ask students to raise their hand if they landed on the exact spot that was described on their card? If they did not land on the spot, ask why this might have happened.

• Discuss how maps were created and what map makers needed to do to ensure accuracy of maps.

Adaptations/Extensions

After students complete this activity, they can create a map of their own.

Standards Addressed

C3. D2.Geo.1.3-5. Construct maps and other graphic representations of both familiar and unfamiliar places.

NCAS. DA:Cr1.1.1 a. Explore movement inspired by a variety of stimuli (e.g., music/sound, text, objects, images, symbols, observed dance, experiences) and identify the source.

References

Berkovich, I. (2020). Conceptualisations of empathy in K-12 teaching: A review of empirical research. *Educational Review, 72*(5), 547–566. https://doi.org/10.1080/00131911.2018.1530196

Borba, M. (2018). Nine competencies for teaching empathy. *Educational Leadership, 76*(2), 22–28.

Council of Chief State School Officers. (2010). *Common Core State Standards for English Language Arts and Literacy in History/Social studies.* CCSSI_ELA Standards.indd (ccsso.org)

Goldberg, M. (2021). *Arts integration: Teaching subject matter through the arts in multicultural settings* (6th ed.). Routledge.

Hardiman, M. (2012). *Brain targeted teaching model for 21st-century schools.* Corwin Press, Inc.

Knight, J. (2015). *Better conversations: Coaching ourselves and each other to be more credible, caring, and connected.* Corwin.

National Council for the Social Studies. (2013). *The C3 Framework for Social Studies State Standards.* https://www.socialstudies.org/standards/c3

Spolin, V. (1963). *Improvisation for the theater: A handbook of teaching and directing techniques* (1st ed.). Northwestern University Press.

Tarlington, C., & Michaels, W. (1995). *Building plays: Simple playbuilding techniques at work.* Pembroke Publishing.

6 Moving Math

Picture This...

Students enter the classroom ready for math class and are presented with a challenge. They are put into groups and tasked with creating a dance that includes and demonstrates the following: (1) a shape (2) balance and imbalance (3) two types of lines (4) symmetry, and (5) over and under, in addition to fitting into 10 counts of 8 of music. Students quickly get to work. They discuss what shape might be best to start the piece and use their bodies to make a circle (see Figure 6.1). They start by using their arms and then one student suggests they try sitting and making it with their legs. Some students start with a square, figuring out how to enact this. Other students discuss how to show balance and imbalance and try out a few moves. Students have fun displaying the over and under challenge with some students making an arch with their arms so that other students can travel under while others make an opening between their legs for students to crawl through. All the while, 25 students are all fully engaged and working diligently, talking about math concepts, using their imaginations and creativity, and collaborating to solve a problem. Sound like math or dance class? This challenge is actually a final exam for a college-level dance program. I have done this activity with hundreds of students in a wide variety of classrooms with varying ages and abilities, and it never disappoints. Students always enjoy this activity and are fully engaged in the learning of both math and dance. In the process, they have all moved their bodies for an extensive amount of time which is not only good for their growing bodies, but essential for transferring these concepts into long-term memory (Hardiman, 2012).

DOI: 10.4324/9781003296317-6

Figure 6.1 Students create a circle shape as they work to create a *math dance* (Photograph taken by author with permission from IAA)

This activity demonstrates many attributes that math and dance have in common. Both rely heavily on patterns, counting, and shapes. On a deeper level, they are also both grounded in problem solving and following order of operations. When I introduce this activity to students, I make these connections clear by explaining what a choreographer does as well as a mathematician, exemplifying the commonalities as well as importance of both sets of skills.

This activity also demonstrates how using the body in the learning of math can be fun, which may help to reduce math anxiety for students. It is widely known that math anxiety is real and a problem for a large portion of students. Many students are concerned about their abilities to learn math, which impacts their engagement, motivation, and performance in math (Luttenberger et al., 2018). There are a multitude of ways to counteract the impact of math anxiety which includes improving self-efficacy, increasing engagement, and altering instructional strategies that are hands-on and enhance students' interest and motivation (Luttenberger et al., 2018). Using fun activities such as the one described can help to reduce math anxiety.

If activities are fun for students, it can help to improve engagement which is the first step toward learning. If students are engaged, they are more likely to understand and learn math concepts. Having activities that help students experience success can improve their self-concept as math learners. This chapter will introduce a variety of ways in which you can engage the body in the learning of math concepts to improve engagement, motivation, and mathematical understanding.

Embodied Cognition and Mathematical Understanding

It is well known that a strong foundation in math is essential for student success in both school and life and yet large portions of US students struggle to reach partial mastery of grade-level knowledge by fourth grade (Erbeli et al., 2021). The use of the body and movement (embodied cognition) has been shown to positively impact learning in math (Fadjo et al., 2009; Glenberg, 2014; Petrick, 2012). Embodied cognition has been discussed repeatedly in this book, but its use in math instruction is particularly impactful and will be explored more fully in this chapter. The use of gestures will also be a focus of this chapter as its use has been proven to improve students' understanding and retention of math concepts (Alibali & Nathan, 2012; Goldin-Meadow et al., 2009; Shapiro & Stolz, 2019; Tran et al., 2017)

Several studies link embodied cognition to mathematical understanding suggesting a strong relationship between perception and action as well as its grounding in the physical environment (Alibali & Nathan, 2012; Glenberg, 2008). According to Glenberg (2014) a leader in the field, embodied cognition is vital to learning all subjects, especially mathematics and science, as they ground abstract concepts in our bodily experiences. Just thinking about how students use their fingers to begin learning basic counting and arithmetic makes this connection clear. Petrick Smith et al. (2014) who studied third and fourth grade students' use of their arms to make and explore concepts of angles found that direct embodiment helps to increase students' understanding of angles. Gerofsky (2011) in her pilot study on the use of the body to conceptualize and explain graphing using the body, what she calls "being the graph," suggests that the use of full-bodied movement improves both engagement and attentiveness to graph instruction compared to just seeing the graph (p. 254).

Use of Gesture to Learn Math Concepts

Gesture or the use of the arms and hands in the learning of math has been shown to help students both learn and retain mathematical understanding (Alibali & Nathan, 2012; Goldin-Meadows et al., 2009; Shapiro & Stolz, 2019; Tran et al., 2017). Using the body to engage with information instead of simply seeing and hearing it can strengthen memory paths because it requires deeper levels of processing which increases retention and makes retrieval easier (Tran et al., 2017). Perhaps the most revealing study to support this was done by Cook et al. (2008) who conducted research on the process of teaching the concept that both sides of an equation must be equal. The researchers taught this concept in three different ways to three sets of children. One group was taught the equalizing strategy using only a verbal cue, repeating after the teacher that one side needed to equal the other. In another group, the students used only gestures, sweeping one hand to the left and then the right to demonstrate the need to have both sides equal. The last group did gestures and speech. While most students made gains on a posttest immediately after instruction, there was a significant difference in how students retained the information. Students who used only verbal cues retained 33% of the concept four weeks later, while those who used gesture or gesture with verbal cues made "robust" gains retaining 85% of their posttest gains (Cook et al., 2008, p. 1053). This finding has significant implications for the use of gesture in education and further supports the use of embodiment in the learning of math.

Use of gestures in the teaching and learning of math has many benefits. It has been shown to lessen students' cognitive load and in doing so frees up some mental space allowing students to better solve problems (Shapiro & Stolz, 2019). Using gestures can also help students communicate what they cannot communicate verbally (Shapiro & Stolz, 2019). This can help to support math learning for students who are ELs, which is vital as classrooms become more diverse. Gesturing can also be used by students to try out ideas and create new ways of thinking (Shapiro & Stolz, 2019; Tran et al., 2017).

Using hand movements in the learning of math concepts, be it pointing at objects, drawing shapes in the air, or creating gestures that articulate a concept helps students to process their learning. Tran et al. (2017) explain that gestures are linked with mathematical understanding and are part of a learning cycle where students both perceive and encode math concepts which guide actions; the outcome of those actions, in turn, guides what is perceived. Since gestures reflect students' embodied thinking about mathematical concepts, they play a crucial role in the communication of learning (Alibali & Nathan, 2012). Therefore, gestures can be helpful in the teaching of math concepts as well as in evaluating students' understanding.

Types of Gestures to Be Used in Math Class

While any use of gesture will help with the learning of math, all gestures are not created equal. The type of gesture you use in your classroom will make a difference. Alibali and Nathan (2012) articulate the types of gestures that can be engaged in learning math, each with their own function and outcomes:

- *Pointing:* Which draws attention to objects like pointing to a line on a graph
- *Iconic:* Shaping the hands into the object like making a bowl or a triangle
- *Metaphorical:* The action conveys a meaning such as two hands out mimicking a scale to show that two sides of an equation need to be balanced/equal

While all gestures make a positive impact on learning and retention, the metaphorical type does require more critical thinking in the process which may improve learning outcomes. Shapiro and Stolz (2019) argue that how students gesture correlates with how well they perform on a certain task and that dynamic gestures (more use of the body versus just fingers) are associated with more advanced understanding (p. 32).

Metaphorical Gestures: Creating Gestures that Convey Meaning

Considering these studies, teachers should work toward using metaphorical gesturing (having students create gestures that demonstrate meaning) that are full bodied and dynamic as they offer the most impact on student learning. Let's take, for example, the gesture previously discussed about using hands to demonstrate that both sides of an equation need to be equal. Students could enact this concept by using their hands, with one hand demonstrating one side, and the other hand demonstrating the other while saying "one side of the equation needs to be equal to the other side." However, using the metaphorical approach would push students further in their gesturing and might include using both hands to mimic a scale to show that both sides need to be balanced. To push this even further, students could be tasked with finding the missing number in an equation using their hands as a scale. For example, if given: $5 + 2 = \_\_ + 1$, students could try out various answers for this missing number, and with each number tried, show what happens to the scale. This use of the body to both explore and express learning will make the concept clearer for students and help greatly with retention. Gestures can be created to explore and express many mathematical concepts. When learning about angles (see Box 6.1), for example, using the arms to create gestures to express the varied types of angles can be helpful. Try making them more dynamic by engaging the whole body (see Figure 6.2)

Gestures for Expressing Mathematical Concepts

Try these gestures for exploring complex math concepts in your active classroom:

Greater than and less than: When making gestures to embody this idea, be sure to explore the notion that when the arms are open wide, they are opening to the bigger number and when gesturing less than, the opposite. This sign has been displayed as an alligator mouth to help young students understand this idea, with the mouth open wide to the bigger number

---

Making Angles

Help students to remember the names of the varying angles by using their bodies. Have students first use their arms, articulating the names of the angles as they gesture: acute, right, and obtuse. Next, put students in pairs and or small groups to explore the other ways their bodies can form these angles (using legs or whole body movements). Have students share. As students observe various groups embodying angles, repeat the names of angles to help reinforce learning.

Box 6.1 Making Angles with Bodies

Figure 6.2 Student uses full body to demonstrate angles, an assignment for a college-level class on arts integration

(as this alligator is very hungry). Having students use this imagery while gesturing would solidify this idea. Encourage students to go further with the idea by having students work in groups of three to demonstrate this concept. Students can find a variety of ways to use their bodies to show the sign as well as how to show one side is greater and one less than.

X & Y coordinates: Try having students embody this idea with arms moving in both directions and saying "X marks the spot" as they reach across the room, and "Y to the sky" as they reach to the ceiling.

Addition, subtraction, & equal signs: When using arms to make models of these symbols, be sure to add some narration to move beyond simply making the sign, but instead add meaning. For example, when taking both arms and crossing them to make an addition sign, have students say, "addition" while adding one arm to the other to make a cross symbol. When making the minus sign with one arm, do a bit of a slicing motion to show you are taking something away (or chopping it) while having students stay: "minus." Have students say "equal sign" at the same time as moving both arms into a parallel position and making them look equal.

Numerator and denominator: To help students remember that the numerator is on top of the line and the denominator is on the bottom, have students do squats while making a deep voice and saying denominator and standing on their tiptoes making a funny high-pitched voice saying numerator. The idea that the denominator is the whole can be explored with the idea of a "hole." Have students mimic digging in the "whole" while saying denominator.

Clockwise and counterclockwise: This is always a tricky concept for students to grasp. Try having students use their arms to mimic the hands of a clock, moving one forward (to the right) to show clockwise and reversing (to the left) to show counter clockwise. Next, have students hold hands making a circle and moving both clockwise and counterclockwise with their groups. Encourage them to create their own movement that demonstrates clockwise and counterclockwise.

Using the Body to Explore and Model Complex Concepts

Embodying mathematical concepts (see Figure 6.3) provides students opportunities to make the abstract more concrete which can support their learning of complex concepts (Tran et al., 2017). Gerofsky (2011), in her recent study of gesture and mathematical understanding, found that abstract mathematical concepts are "grounded in our physical, embodied experiences of the world" (p. 246). In her pilot study on gesture and graphing, students were asked to describe graphs that were presented on cards using non-technical terms and gestures as if they were explaining it to someone who could not see them. Unlike the study done by Cook et al. (2008), students were able to use their own form of gesture, as it was not taught to them in any specific way. Results suggest that students may benefit from using kinesthetic whole-body movement when attempting to understand complex mathematical concepts, as well as demonstrating more "engagement and attentiveness" (Gerofsky, 2011, p. 254). Another study found that students who acted out the story in word problems were more likely to answer problems correctly (Sparks, 2011). (See Box 6.2 for directions for acting out word problems.)

"Acting out" Math Concepts

There are many math concepts that would benefit from using the body more fully in the learning process. These activities provide students the opportunity to experience concepts with their bodies, making them more tangible. They also provide a visual representation of the ideas that aid in the learning process. Before you get started acting out math concepts, warm students up with the *math shakedown* (Box 6.3).

Figure 6.3 Students make a square using their bodies
(Photograph taken by author with permission from IAA)

Adding and Subtracting: Even concepts as simple as adding and subtracting can be better understood when using the body in the process. Consider having students sit in a circle, asking one student to stand in the middle. Ask students to choose a number to add. As this number is chosen, the exact number of students are asked to join. As this occurs, write the equation on the board to

Word Problems in Action

Try having students put their acting and improvisation skills learned in previous chapters to work in math class. Give students number sentences such as (2 + 2 = 4 or 5 − 3 = 2). In groups, ask them to create a word problem scene to bring these math equations to a real-world setting. For example, if getting the equation 5 − 4 = 1, students might act out an amazing race where the first person drops out because it's just too far, the second breaks their ankle, the third sees a friend and decides to hang with them instead, and the fourth goes the wrong way. In the end, one person makes it to the finish line. While doing this activity, the numbers will be small because of optimal working group sizes (and easiest to focus on subtraction and addition). However, the goal of the lesson is to focus on the real-world connection of math and how word problems simply tell a story about math concepts

Box 6.2 Acting Out Word Problems

offer both a kinesthetic and visual representation of what is occurring. Once you get all the students in the circle, you can begin the subtraction process until there are no students standing. Add more fun and movement to this activity by adding a specific movement to the activity. For example, if one student goes to the middle, they can choose an action like hopping on one foot or marching. As each set of students is added to the group, they mimic this action. You can even vocalize this to lay the groundwork for word problems. "There is one student

Math Shake Down

A simple way to get students moving during math class is to have students do an action that aligns with the number chosen. For example, jump ten times (and count while doing so). Try other movements such as hop on one leg, clap, wiggle, squat, or ask students to suggest movements. Try making a pattern with all the suggestions: 10 jumps, 2 claps, 10 jumps, 2 claps. Find a way to draw this pattern on the board with shapes to make the pattern more visual as well as kinesthetic.

Box 6.3 Counting and Movement Warm Up

marching. We added ten more kids and now there are 11 students marching." Each student who begins each "problem" can choose their own action.

Decomposing numbers: In a similar activity as above, explore the notion of decomposing. Show pictures of what happens in the decomposing process of breaking down matter (nice connection to science). Have a group of students (for example, six) stand in the middle of the circle. Ask for volunteers to "break down" this big number into smaller parts. As this is done, students split up according to the numbers suggested. Be sure to write equations on the board as this is done, as you work as a class to both physicalize and notate all the ways a number can be decomposed. (See how this activity can be done with *number bonds*, Box 6.4.)

Human Number Bond

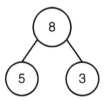

Use masking tape to create a visual of a number bond on the floor, making sure it is big enough for at least six people to fit inside. Ask six students to stand in the top circle. Ask them to explore all the ways that six can be decomposed into the other two circles. Physicalizing this concept makes it more clear what it means to break down these numbers in a variety of ways. Add more fun/movement to this practice. After you have modeled this process once. Put students in groups of four, five, or six. Ask them to create a movement series to exemplify this process. (It's easiest to move from the smaller numbers to the larger as it demonstrates how the two combine to make the larger number.) For example, if the total number is four, students could show three people in one circle who do three claps, and one person in the other circle does one jump. Then they move into the top circle and put them all together which results in a movement series: three claps and one jump to make four. Each group makes a movement series to demonstrate all their combinations and present for the group. (Adding music can make it extra fun!)

Box 6.4 Human Number Bonds with Movement

Division and multiplication: The idea of fractions can also be embodied similarly to the decomposing numbers activity. However, there is a bit of a shift in the language. Start with the whole class in the middle of the room. Be sure to write that number on the board. Explain that you want to know all the ways this group can be broken up evenly. For example, if there are 24 students, ask for a volunteer to suggest a number that could be used to break up 24 evenly. If the student says "6," ask students to break up into 6 groups. When they have done so, ask them to count how many are in each group. Write this equation on the board while vocalizing 24 students can be divided into 6 groups of 4. If the next student volunteers the number 5, have them try to do this. When it doesn't work evenly and you have a few kids searching for a group with no luck, call "freeze". Ask students to explain what happened and name what these last few kids without a group would be called? They are the remainders or who remain after groups have been broken up evenly.

Perimeter and area: Students often confuse these two terms/ideas. To help students distinguish between the two, have them use their bodies to explore these ideas. Ask students to work in groups of four and visualize a square on the ground. Have one student walk around this space using their feet to "measure" it by saying: "perimeter, I am walking around this spaces' perimeter." Have the other students use their bodies to fill up the area by saying "we are filling this entire area." This can be done more effectively outside, using chalk to fill in the area and having all students walk the perimeter of the object drawn.

Lesson Plans to Explore Complex Concepts Using Movement (at the end of this chapter)

> *Square dance*
> *Moving multiplication*
> *Twirling 2s*
> *Exploring symmetry*
> *Line dance*

Human Models

One way to embody math concepts and make abstract concepts more concrete is to create human models. Have students create these math models using movement:

Bar graph: Have students make a human bar graph. Start by polling students on a certain question such as favorite ice-cream (identify the choices as chocolate, vanilla, strawberry, or other) or favorite animals such as dog, cat, or fish. After showing a picture of a bar graph on the board, have students make rows on the floor as they choose their favorite item. Once students are in place, do some counting and comparing. As you compare numbers in lines, ask students to reach across to another row and connect to another student. This way you can easily count how many more are in a row/category. As you work to do comparisons, you are reiterating the language of more than and less than. This vocalizing of terms repeatedly will reinforce these concepts and terms: "How many more students like chocolate ice cream?" "Which group has the most?" "Which has the least?" To make this activity even more active and fun, ask each group to come up with a move to represent their choice. For example, for the group that chooses dogs, maybe they do a dog tail waggle or the cats make a claw and say "meow". Each time you call out that group, students do the move.

Human number line: A common mistake with number lines is that students often count 1 on the first line (which is meant to represent zero). By making a physical number line in your classroom (or outside on the playground using chalk), students can experience that the second line represents 1. This becomes clear as you ask students to count as they move forward on the line. For example, they have to count one to move from the first line to the second. Next, have students move along the number line as you call out numbers and actions, having them count as they move (jump 4, step 5, leap 2, etc.). Students can line up and follow the leader through the maze of number lines. Play a game moving forward and back to find their product. "March 5 spaces forward, take away 2 (moving back), what number do you get?"

Plotting lines: Use chalk to make graphs in an outdoor space (even 12 × 12 will work). Start by giving students cards that have x, y coordinates listed and have them find these spots on the graph. Next, put students into groups of four or five. Task them with coming up with the coordinates that make a straight line, modeling this with their bodies on the graph.

Human arrays: Making arrays is a key concept in elementary math. Having students build them with their bodies is a great way to have students experience first-hand how these work and get them up and moving during math class. Write number problems on the board and ask for volunteers to stand in rows to represent blocks.

MOVING MATH LESSON PLANS

"Square" Dance (Exploring Shapes)

Grades K and 1 (content)
Grades 2–6 (collaboration & creative problem solving)

In this fun and active lesson, students will work in groups to explore creating shapes with their classmates. Students will experience the creative process and one way that a dance is created by choreographers. This can be used in a math lesson to learn and explore with shapes or as an activity in any classroom to practice collaboration and creative problem solving.

What You Will Need

- An open space
- Music
- Cards with shapes on them—or other visuals

Student Learning Objective

Students will work in groups to create a movement piece that explores and demonstrates the creation of shapes including lines, circles, and the changing of dimensions.

How to Do the Activity

1. Start with a warm- up: Ask students to make one large circle. Ask students to begin by individually making any shape with their bodies (This can be anything—not a typical shape they know). Ask them to make a second (and different shape) and then a third. Ask students to make a high shape and one that is low. Now ask them to make a shape that is in the middle (medium height.) Ask students to make a small shape and then a big one. Ask students to make the widest shape they can and now the thinnest. Explain that today's lesson will be on both math and dance—understanding and making shapes in effort to create an engaging dance piece. They will be called upon to be both mathematicians (people who solve math problems) and choreographers (people who make dances).
2. Divide students into groups of three or four depending on their experience of working in groups.

3. Give students cards with different shapes (or have some examples of shapes on the board).
4. Give students 5–10 minutes to choose 4–5 shapes and make the shapes with group members.
5. Play music and allow students to explore and create on their own.
6. After about 10 minutes, announce that the students have an additional requirement. They must now take these basic shapes that they have created and put them together to create a dance (or movement piece). Explain that choreographers use various ideas to inspire their work, and that now they will take their first set of ideas—the shapes they created—and use it as the pieces of their dance. (A nice analogy here is the sentence: The shapes are the words and now they need to create a sentence stringing a few words together to make something that makes sense.) Students must figure out how to move from one shape to another, choose the order of the shapes, and define a beginning, middle, and end to their piece making artistic choices just like choreographers do. Give students 10–15 more minutes and announce that they will share their pieces at the end of that time period.
7. Do some sidecoaching—pushing then to explore each shape, asking: "How could this shape move; or get bigger, smaller, or change slightly?"—to help them be more creative with their explorations.
8. Students share their work. Explain that the job of the audience is to identify the shapes they see, the beginning, middle, and end of the piece, and any feeling that the dance communicates to them.

Standard Addressed

CCSS.MATH.CONTENT.K.G.B.5 Model shapes in the world by building shapes from components (e.g., sticks and clay balls) and drawing shapes.

Note: While this is identified as a K standard, it can be adapted easily as review for older grades, to explore and identify more features of shapes, or to explore three-dimensional shapes.

NCAS. DA:Pr4.1.K. a. Make still and moving body shapes that show lines (for example, straight, bent, and curved), changing levels, and vary in size (large/small). Join with others to make a circle formation and work with others to change its dimensions.

Math Groupings and Remainders

Grade K-5

This activity can be used in a variety of ways. It can be used to creatively group students, readying them for doing an activity in groups, as a review of math skills, or to learn new math concepts. Having students move into groups will help all students visualize what it means to group numbers: adding, subtracting, and basic multiplying and how certain groups will divide equally and some will not, leaving remainders. This game can be easily tailored to the math level of your group.

What You Need

- Open space
- Some math challenges ready

Student Objectives

Students work collaboratively to solve math problems, demonstrating fluently in adding and subtracting within 1000 and the multiplication of single digits.

How to Do the Activity

1. Tell students that you will be calling out number problems. When they have solved the problem, they must make groups of that number without talking or "grabbing" people to join them.
2. Practice: Teacher might say: "For example, if I say two plus two, you will make groups of 4 following the rules: be safe in the space, no talking, and you must form the numbers as quickly as possible with the student closest to you."
3. Depending on the level of the students, read out math problems asking students to make groupings of the product. (To place some kind of time limit on the game, you may call out 10 seconds to complete each problem, beat 10 on the drum, or play and stop music.)
4. When you reach the level of multiplication, write the number of students on the board. Ask students to pick a number that they think this number could be evenly divided into. Try to make these groups, and see what number of students are in each group. Write this equation on the board. Find all the numbers that the total

number can be divided into. Discuss what it means when the group cannot be evenly divided and the meaning of remainders. (List what numbers can be made without remainders on the board for the number of total students in the game.)

Helpful Hint

Review the basic two rules of creative work: (1) Try everything and (2) no hurting each other physically or emotionally. Discuss what it would mean to not let one student join your group, but instead pull in a "friend" and how this might affect that student's feelings and the class community.

Adaptation/Extensions

To create groups: This activity can also be used to make groups for activities. Many of the activities in this book ask for groups to be made before playing the game. This is a fun, active, and strategic way to mix the class up and not allow friends to always end up together in groups.

Combing with statues: Once students get into groups, you can give them other math challenges such as show greater than/less than, make shapes, or other gestures for math concepts. You can also give them written math challenges that they can work on as a group.

Standards Addressed

CCSS.MATH.CONTENT.3.NBT.A.2 Fluently add and subtract within 1000 using strategies and algorithms based on place value, properties of operations, and/or the relationship between addition and subtraction.

CCSS.MATH.CONTENT.3.NBT.A.3 Multiply one-digit whole numbers by multiples of 10 in the range 10–90 (e.g., 9×80, 5×60) using strategies based on place value and properties of operations.

Exploring Symmetry

Grades K-6

In this simple exercise, students explore the facets of symmetry. Students use a theater exercise called "mirrors" to explore how a mirror works to create symmetry. Students create symmetrical sculptures to demonstrate their understanding of this concept.

What You Need

- Open space
- Music

Student Learning Objective

Students will participate in a cognitive exercise that is used to build drama skills, and in doing so, recognize and demonstrate a line of symmetry and two identical parts.

How to Do the Activity

1. Show a few examples of an object that is symmetrical.
2. Put students in pairs.
3. Have students face each other, putting their hands up in front of their chests and hands palm to palm almost touching.
4. Tell students to imagine they are using a mirror and must mirror their partners' moves exactly.
5. Give time for each student to be the leader and follower.
6. Ask what they notice about the "picture" they create?
7. Explain that this is symmetry (that the "mirror" represents the line of symmetry).
8. Next have students work with their partner to create three symmetrical statues.
9. Ask them to find a way to move from one to the other- add music
10. Share with the group.

Reflect and Wrap Up

What did students notice about the various statues created? How would they define symmetry?

Standards Addressed

   CCSS.MATH.CONTENT.4.G.A.3 Recognize a line of symmetry for a two-dimensional figure as a line across the figure such that the figure can be folded along the line into matching parts. Identify line-symmetric figures and draw lines of symmetry.
   NCAS. TH:Pr5.1.3.a. Participate in a variety of physical, vocal, and cognitive exercises that can be used in a group setting for drama/theater work.

Living Lines

Grades 2–6

Students work in groups to explore the various types of lines that exist while working like choreographers who use lines often to create dances.

What You Need

- Open space
- Music

Student Learning Objective

Students create lines, line segments, perpendicular and parallel lines in groups while demonstrating a range of locomotor movements, body patterning, and dance sequences that require moving through space using a variety of pathways.

How to Do the Activity

1. Share visuals that contain the various kinds of lines: parallel, perpendicular, and diagonal.
2. Show pictures of various dance pieces that demonstrate the use of lines in dance such as the Rockettes.
3. Ask students to work in groups of 4–5 to use their bodies to make the various kinds of lines
4. Have students now use those lines as a building block for a dance piece by choosing a way to move from one line to the next in a fluid and creative way and a way to move while in each line formation (for example, a kick line, or wave, etc.).
5. Perform for the group asking observers to identify the lines seen and choices made to articulate them.

Reflect and Wrap Up

Ask students to identify the lines witnessed and respond to choices made in the dances. What did they notice and wonder? Ask students to describe the use of lines for creating dance works and how math can be articulated in real world situations.

Standards Addressed

CCSS.MATH.CONTENT.4.G.A.1 Draw points, lines, line segments, rays, angles (right, acute, obtuse), and perpendicular and parallel lines. Identify these in two-dimensional figures.

NCAS. DA:Pr5.1.2.a. Demonstrate a range of locomotor and non-locomotor movements, body patterning, and dance sequences that require moving through space using a variety of pathways.

Multiplication Square Dance

Grades 2–6

Get kids up and moving to this fun "take" on the traditional square dance that embodies the concepts of multiplication. Students can visual and physicalize how multiplication works through this active way to group numbers.

What You Need

- Open space
- Hoedown music such as Turkey in the Straw

How to Do the Activity

1. It would be helpful to do the Hoedown activity in Chapter 5 (box 5.3) to set the tone for this activity which has students learn about a hoedown and how to respond to a caller.
2. Next, have students listen to the chosen song for this activity—identifying the beat and counting by 4s. Ask students to clap along and count each group of 4; for example, 1,2,3,4 then 2,2,3,4, 3,2,3,4, etc. Ask students to identify how many counts of 4 are in the chorus, using their skills to do multiplication—for example, how many groups of 4? Write this equation on the board.
3. Next, have students make two lines facing each other, each student having a partner across from them which makes a pair (the first group in the line will be called "the 2s"), each group called after will be called "pairs"; as you do the dance, you keep adding a pair of students (going down the line).

4. Teach students how to do-si-do and swing their partner (steps described in Hoedown activity, Chapter 5).
5. Begin the calling as such:

Dance Calls

- Now the 2's step forward (i.e., first pair) now do-si-do. 2, 1 time, 2×1 is 2.
- Now the 2's step forward, add one more pair. 2, 2 times, $2 \times 2 = 4$.
- Now swing your partners round and round, have some fun, and bring it on home.
- Now the 2's step forward, add 2 more pairs, 2, 3 times, $2 \times 3 = 6$.
- Now do-si-do–now bring it on home.

Continue until all pairs have participated. Go back between do-si-do and swing your partner; adding that call in between calling new pairs to join.

Standards Addressed

CCSS.MATH.CONTENT.3.OA.A.1 Interpret products of whole numbers, e.g., interpret 5×7 as the total number of objects in five groups of seven objects each. *For example, describe a context in which a total number of objects can be expressed as 5×7.*
NCAS. DA:Cr2.1.PK b. Engage in dance experiences moving alone or with a partner.

Twirling 2s

Grades K-1

In this fun movement activity, students practice counting by 2s and work with a partner to create their own movements that are combined to create a collective dance.

What you need

- Open space
- Music

Student Learning Objective

Students demonstrate their understanding of the relationship between numbers and cardinality by responding in movement to music.

How to Do the Activity

1. Pair students
2. Ask each pair to stand together, making two lines with all students in the classroom clearly demonstrating the groupings: (Notice students are arranged with spaces in between pairs (called "windows" in theater, so all children can be seen.)

    XX   XX XX XX XX XX XX
    XX XX XX
      XX XX XX

3. Assign an order to your pairs so that when you call out each set of 2's they know when to move (for example: first pair are the "2s," second pair is the "4," third pair is "6," and so on.)
4. Tell students that the first "move" when called will be to stand and wave their arms back and forth. As you count by 2s (with students counting out loud with you), each group stands at the given time and waves their arms. For example: 2,4,6,8 (and as you call out each number that group stands and waves).
5. Pick a second move like turning/twirling, etc. Repeat the process above with this new move.
6. Next, have pairs come up with their own move together so when their number is called, they do their own original movement.
7. Complete the whole dance in order, beginning with stand and wave, twirl, and finally with their own moves.

Extension/Adaptations

This can be adapted for any number, i.e., groups of 3 (with 3 students), 4s, or 5s. As you change the number, you will make groupings with that number (i.e., counting by 3s, have groups of 3). It is easier to accomplish this with smaller groups.

Standards Addressed

CCSS.MATH.CONTENT.K.CC.B.4 Understand the relationship between numbers and quantities; connect counting to cardinality.

NCAS. DA:Cr1.1.K a. Respond in movement to a variety of stimuli (for example, music/sound, text, objects, images, symbols, and observed dance).

References

Alibali, M. W., & Nathan, M. J. (2012). Embodiment in mathematics teaching and learning: Evidence from learners and teachers' gestures. *Journal of the Learning Sciences, 21*(2), 247–286. https://doi.org/10.1080/10508406.2011.611446

Cook, S. W., Mitchell, A., & Goldin-Meadow, S. (2008). Gesturing makes learning last. *Cognition, 106*(2), 1047–1058. https://doi.org/10.1016/j.cognition.2007.04.010

Erbeli, F., Shi, Q., Campbell, A. R., Hart, S. A., & Woltering, S. (2021). Developmental dynamics between reading and math in elementary school. *Developmental Science, 24*(1), e13004. https://doi-org.ezproxy.uvm.edu/10.1111/desc.13004

Fadjo, C. L., Ming-Tsan, P. L., & Black, J. B. (2009, June 22). *Instructional embodiment and video game programming in an after school program.* Paper presented at EdMedia + Innovate Learning, Honolulu, HI. https://www.learntechlib.org/primary/p/32064/

Gerofsky, S. (2011). Seeing the graph vs. being the graph: Gesture, engagement and awareness in school mathematics. In G. Stam, & M. Ishino (Eds.), *Integrating gestures* (pp. 245–256). John Benjamins Publishing.

Glenberg, A. (2008). Embodiment for education. In P. Calvo, & T. Gomila (Eds.), *Handbook of cognitive science: An embodied approach* (pp. 355–372). Elsevier.

Glenberg, A. (2014, July 22). How acting out in schools boosts learning. *Scientific American.* http://www.scientificamerican.com/article/how-acting-out-in-school-boosts-learning/

Goldin-Meadow, S., Cook, S. W., & Mitchell, Z. A. (2009). Gesturing gives children new ideas about math. *Psychological Science, 20*(3), 267–272. https://doi.org/10.1111/j.1467-9280.2009.02297.x

Hardiman, M. M. (2012). *Brain targeted teaching model for 21st-century schools.* Corwin.

Luttenberger, S., Wimmer, S., & Paechter, M. (2018). Spotlight on math anxiety. *Psychology Research and Behavior Management, 11,* 311–322. https://doi.org/10.2147/PRBM.S141421

Petrick, C. J. (2012). *Every body move: Learning mathematics through embodied actions.* [Doctoral dissertation, University of Texas].

Petrick Smith, C., King, B., & Hoyte, J. (2014). Learning angles through movement: Critical actions for developing understanding in an embodied activity. *The Journal of Mathematical Behavior, 36,* 95–108.

Shapiro, L., & Stolz, S. A. (2019). Embodied cognition and its significance for education. *Theory and Research in Education, 17*(1), 19–39. https://doi.org/10.1177/1477878518822149

Sparks, S. D. (2011). "Acting out" text found to promote pupils' learning. *Education Week, 30*(36), 18.

Tran, C., Smith, B., & Buschkuehl, M. (2017). Support of mathematical thinking through embodied cognition: Nondigital and digital approaches. *Cognitive Research, 2,* 16. https://doi-org.ezproxy.uvm.edu/10.1186/s41235-017-0053-8

7 Science in Motion
Don't Lose STEAM!

Picture This...

When students enter the classroom, Newton's first law of motion is written on the board: "The Law of Inertia: An object at rest remains at rest, and an object in motion remains in motion at a constant speed and in a straight line unless acted on by an unbalanced force." The goal of the lesson is explained to the students. They will create a dramatic scene that demonstrates the idea of inertia. Students quickly get to work. One scene depicts a mom and a young child who doesn't want to go to school, and the child sits motionless. The mom tries multiple ways to impose force, first by poking and prodding and next by "dragging" the child out the door. The students all laugh at this silly rendition of this concept. Another pair depicts a scene about two young people, one of which won't move from their TV-watching daze. One student sits motionless on the couch zoned out watching their favorite program, while the friend tries various means to motivate them to go outside and play. In another lesson, students work in pairs to model the second part of this law, finding ways to demonstrate the idea that an object will stay in motion unless acted on by an unbalanced force. One pair shows a student walking across the room and as their partner steps in their path, it causes the first student to move in a new direction. This mimics a modern dance piece as they continue to play with this idea, creating new patterns of movement. In a second lesson, students use movement to demonstrate the types of motion, using the classroom as a dance studio as they move across the floor finding a multitude of ways to show: push, pull, drag, etc. (See lesson plan *Force and Motion* at the end of the chapter.) At the end of

DOI: 10.4324/9781003296317-7

this unit, I gave students a survey to discuss their experiences using these techniques to explore science concepts, and one student expressed that she would have never been able to understand or remember these ideas if they hadn't used movement to explore them more fully. For her, the terms and language of the laws were too confusing. Students' engagement in these lessons and their abilities to demonstrate their understanding of complex concepts using movement and theater reinforced how important it is to engage the whole body when learning science. This chapter will share some ways in which you can engage students in the learning of science using movement and theater.

Embodied Cognition and the Use of Gesture in the Learning of Science

As has been repeated throughout this book, the use of the body in the learning process (embodied cognition, including the use of gestures) greatly impacts student learning. Its use in the learning of science is no exception. Similar to math, the study of science includes many complex concepts that are difficult to visualize. Having students engage with these ideas in physical ways, such as making human models or using gestures (see Figure 7.1) as well as "acting out" ideas, can help students more deeply engage with content as well as improve understanding and retention (Glenberg, 2014). As Glenberg (2014) has argued: "The theory of embodied cognition also tells us that the abstractions that are important for language, mathematics, physics, and so on, are understood by grounding or mapping the abstract material onto our bodily experiences" (para 6).

Research on embodied cognition in the learning of scientific concepts affirms what the student expressed in the survey about using dance to learn Newton's laws of motion, that using movement helped her understand complex concepts like inertia. Glenberg (2014) argues that concepts like centrifugal force cannot be truly understood unless it is experienced physically. The equation for centripetal force, he suggests, requires simulation to understand how velocity, force, mass, and radius act together. He shares a study where college students act out the equation, changing the rope length to test out the relationship, and in doing so helped them disprove a common misconception that increasing length would increase force.

Figure 7.1 Preservice teachers use physicalization to create a human model of the water cycle.

Glenberg argues that all classrooms should utilize more physical activity to help students understand abstract concepts.

In a study that tested the effect that EMRELE (Embodied Mixed Reality Learning Environment) had on two high school science studies, Johnson-Glenberg et al. (2014) found that students who were able to experience learning supplemented by EMRELE, which was multi-modal and highly physical, showed learning gains compared to those in science classes that used traditional instructional methods. The researchers hypothesized that the opportunities for collaboration and the highly engaged physical embodiment were responsible for increased learning. Roth (2001), in her review of studies on gesture when used in the teaching and learning of science, found that gesture helped students construct knowledge, particularly with complex concepts where students lack the vocabulary and language to explain things verbally. Roth describes a study in which students attempt to explain concepts of force and motion using computer simulation and gesture (without the adequate science vocabulary yet acquired) and found

Do Opposites Really Attract? Particles Greeting

Explain how protons, electrons, and neutrons function and that there is a magnetic attraction that binds them in an atom. Explain the idea of attraction and repelling in regard to positive and negatively charged particles. Use small circle stickers and give half the students one color to symbolize a proton (explaining that it has a positive charge) and the other half another color sticker to symbolize an electron that has a negative change. Play music. When the music stops, ask students to "bind' with a particle that has an opposite charge. As they do, they greet this partner. Repeat three times so students can greet different students. (See lesson plan: *Protons, Neutrons, and Atoms* at the end of this chapter for full lesson.)

Box 7.1 Particles Greeting

that the use of gesture was effective and may help students "develop scientific modes of discourse" more quickly than when gesture is not used. This is important in today's diverse classrooms as it can support students who are ELs during their transitional stages of language acquisition (Roth, 2001, pp. 375–378). While these studies are conducted with older students, the notion that they would be equally and possibly more effective with elementary-age children is easy to assume. Young children are curious, active, and may have more trouble visualizing complex concepts. Using movement (be it theater or dance) as an instructional strategy for teaching science has proven to improve student retention of content, which makes it a valuable pedagogy for science instruction (Hardiman, et. al, 2019). Additionally, giving students positive experiences in science learning at a young age could support the development of a life-long love of science. Get things started right-try beginning science class or morning meeting with a fun and science inspired greeting (see Box 7.1).

Lessons from the Renaissance: Science and Art Are More Similar than Different

While learning in science and the arts have been separated in school settings, they haven't always been. In the Renaissance period, considered a revolutionary time for both science and art, many of our greatest thinkers and innovators were dedicated to both bodies of knowledge. Consider Vitruvian Man created by Leonardo da Vinci that is a clear integration of both scientific and artistic concepts. It is a work of art that has been admired and studied by many for its artistic qualities and it also demonstrates the ideal proportion of the human body. Da Vinci declared that to paint nude poses, one had to study anatomy to create realistic looking bodies. Filippo Brunelleschi, one of the most famous and prolific architects of the Renaissance period, displayed his attention to art, science, and mathematics in his creation of the majestic beamless cupola of the Florence Dome. In 1427, he created the painting "The Trinity," which utilized the scientific concept of perspective for the first time which transformed the art of painting (Tonelli, 2013).

A recent educational push for STEAM learning versus simply STEM is built on this premise that the arts should be integrated with the studies of science, math, engineering, and technology. Despite its catchy phrase, it seems to have lost *steam* in the school reform movement. There is, however, much to be gained when the arts are combined with a study of science which will be explored more fully in this chapter.

Similarities in the Scientific Process and the Creative Process

At their core, the scientific method and the creative process (creating a new work of art) are actually quite similar (see Figure 7.2). Both move through a process that starts with curiosity, making guesses about how something works or could work, collecting data and information to help illuminate the question, exploring the question through various means, and ending with the sharing of findings or the results of inquiry. Burnaford et al. (2001) documented the outcomes of the Chicago Arts Partnership in Education (CAPE) program that integrated the arts with all subjects, including science. They argue that the goal of both science and art are to make sense of the world and follow a process of observing, exploring relationships and patterns, and communicating ideas:

> Although the scientific process, with its emphasis on empirical, quantifiable evidence, is the conventional image, much of science is also found in breakthroughs of insight. Deciding what to study, which data to gather, and

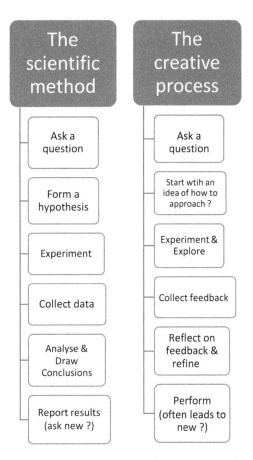

Figure 7.2 Chart comparing the similarities of the scientific and artistic processes (Visual created by the author)

> what sense to make of the data often involves scientific insights that are just as intuitive as analytical. Many scientists consider the aspect of their work involved in coming up with original ideas to be like that of art, the *eureka!* effect functions in both.
>
> (Burnaford et al., 2001, p. 138)

Both processes begin with defining a problem. In the scientific process, this might be a question such as what factors contribute to making water boil faster. In the creative process, this question might be something like, how can I express the complexity of experiences around having dyslexia using dance so that others can more fully understand its impact. This inquiry was articulated in the dance work "In search of air: Growing up dyslexic" by Lida Winfield. She used both storytelling and physicalization to express what it felt like to have dyslexia and navigate schooling in K-12 education (https://youtu.be/oilizJq-HLw). The next stage in the scientific process is to form a hypothesis, which isn't much different from the next stage of the creative process which starts with a "hunch," or the first idea about how to approach the exploration of the driving question. In both the scientific and creative process, the next stage is exploration—trying different things. In the case of the boiling water experiment, the scientist might try adding varying substances to the water such as salt or sugar. They might test out different temperatures or heat sources. For the artist, they might try out various techniques, styles of dance, types of storytelling, or a combination of the two. The artist may try out different ways to begin the story or ways to approach the process. The artist is searching for the best way to express what they are exploring. Both processes end with a sharing of findings and discoveries. For the scientist, it might be a journal article or conference presentation and for the artist it could be an exhibit or performance. Both the artist and scientist often ask for feedback, which may lead to more questions, hypotheses or avenues for further discovery, or clarity on the question or problem. There are a few key ways that the arts are particularly linked with science which make the teaching of them in tandem effective. This includes how dancers are experts about the body, both bodies of knowledge start with curiosity, and observation is key to both studies. Each idea will be explored more fully in the next section.

Dancers and the Body

Dancers are experts about the body. They must understand how the body works in effort to manipulate it to its fullest. Just considering how Martha Graham used the body to tell a story, how Alvin Ailey pushed the body to its athletic limits, and how Bob Fosse twerked the body in new ways, demonstrates how choreographers use the body as a tool. Using dance in a science classroom is a way to have students both explore with and learn about the body and retain what they have learned.

This was experienced first-hand when working in a third-grade class-room a few years back. They were learning the parts of the body in their science class. To align with this study, students engaged in a choreography

Move Those Muscles Warm Up

Try creating a warm up for your science class that names and uses the main muscles in the body in a similar way that a dancer warms up the body to prepare for their work. It is easiest to start from the top of the body, starting with the neck and working your way down to the ankles. As you do so, name the muscles in play. For example, begin by stretching the *sternocleidomastoid* and *trapezius* muscles by turning the head left and right then rotating making a half circle forward. Move to the *deltoid* and *trapezius* muscles by rolling the shoulders forward and back, shrugging, and making big arm circles. Next, have students stretch the arms out and back (curling forearms in and out) while saying *biceps* and *triceps*. Twist the torso leaning right and left saying *oblique* muscle. Do squats and bend and straighten the legs while saying *quadriceps*. Stretch the *hamstrings* by putting an ankle out stretching down to touch toes. Finish off with some ankle rotations saying *tibialis anterior*. (This is a short list. Many more can be added depending on the age of students and learning goals.)

Box 7.2 Moving Muscle Warm Up

unit during their theater class. When I inquired about what they had already learned, in effort to build upon it, the teacher expressed that they had already covered the main muscles in the body and should be able to name them. In the next class, I introduced a full body warm up in which the main muscles would be recounted, and only 1 or 2 students out of the 24 could name a muscle. It was shocking. Moving forward, we created a warm-up where students said the muscle out loud and then manipulated it (see Box 7.2). For example, when students said "quadricep" they did a squat and pointed to that muscle. We worked our way through some of the key muscles in the body in this same way. This was how we started our class each day. After repeating this short exercise for a few weeks, almost all of the students could easily name the key muscles in the body.

Following Curiosity: Inquiry in Science and Art

Perhaps the strongest link between the study of science and the study of the arts (with a focus here on theater and dance) is that both are grounded in curiosity.

As Goldberg (2021) has articulated: "The overlap between the world of the scientist and artist is strikingly similar, and learning the processes involved with each discipline will strengthen the work of each; scientists and artists often share a fundamental curiosity and desire to understand the wonders of nature" (p. 150). This curiosity drives inquiry. For the scientist, inquiry begins with wonder about how things work, which drives experiments. Wonder is also at the source of creative work. An artist, for example, may wonder about how to capture the colors in the night sky, how to explore an emotion through a dance work, or how to demonstrate a complex relationship through a dramatic scene. In both schools of thought, a question drives the scientist/artist toward inquiry, investigation, exploration, and discovery.

Theater and Observation Skills

One of the key ways that theater can support learning in science is by teaching observation skills. To be a scientist, one must have keen observation skills. The scientist must look closely at the object of study and pay attention to changes as they occur. Think of the student who studies the growth of a plant from seed to flower. At each stage, the student scientist needs to make careful notes of what they observe and notice any and all details about the changing subject. Theater is a great way to teach observation skills because it is a visual artform. It is not just the words spoken on stage (the script) that provide the story in a theatrical work, but the set, the lighting, the body language of the actors as well as the staging of the script (how actors move on stage in relation to each other and the set). The theater goer must closely observe these visual aspects in effort to make sense of the story. Because of this, the actor's training is grounded in the physical body. They learn to use their body as well as their voice to communicate on stage: the shrug of a shoulder, the darting eye, the slight tilt of the head. All physical movements are clues to what the actor is trying to portray about their feelings, which in some cases aligns with the script and sometimes is in contrast. Therefore, actors must also develop their observation skills. They need to be keenly aware of all things happening on stage especially in regard to their fellow actors. Actors who work together in a scene must closely observe their partner's physical cues to respond accordingly to be unified in their storytelling efforts. Improvisation, a key theater skill, depends on the actor's skills at both seeing and picking up on cues of their partner.

Change Three Things

As a quick warm up or a way to teach the importance of observation, try this fun activity. One student changes three things about their appearance with classmates tasked with guessing what was changed. The game starts with one volunteer who stands in the center of the circle. Classmates are given three minutes to observe this student's physical appearance. After a few minutes, this student leaves the room and changes three things. They might untie one shoelace, roll up their sleeves, or remove a hat. The foundational rule in this game is that the change has to be clearly visible. As the student reenters the circle, classmates guess about what changes were made.

Box 7.3 Change Three Things Game to Practice Observation Skills

They react in the moment as their partner gives clues to *who, what, and where* they are (see "Improvisation 101" discussion in Chapter 3). Throughout this book, the role of the observer is paramount to the learning process. Students are asked to observe the work of their classmates and make connections, comments, and respond to the work. Doing so will strengthen your students in the skill of observation and in their abilities to articulate clearly what they observe. Have students play *Change Three Things Game* (Box 7.3) to practice their observation skills as well as other observation activities introduced in earlier chapters.

Other Lessons to Practice Observation Skills (all in Chapter 3).

- *My Journey Today*
- *Freeze*
- *Diamonds*

Example of an Inquiry Science Lesson that Is Integrated with Movement to Explore How Animals Work Together to Survive

The following excerpt shares details about a lesson that integrates movement with a science lesson on animal interdependence. This is shared to help give a better picture of how this process could work in your classroom and act as a model for other ways to integrate movement into science learning. Using an inquiry, 5 Es, model, the lesson seeks to begin by spurring students' curiosity.

- *Engage:* Begin the lesson with a driving question that can be used as a catalyst for the learning such as: "In what ways do animals work together in the wild that helps them survive?" Ask students to share any examples that they can identify and a list of both ideas and questions are noted.
- *Explore and Explain:* Allow students to explore through movement the various ways that animals work together to survive:
  - *Penguin huddles:* The first exploration is about penguins. Students are shown a short video about how penguins work together in a systematic way to keep warm, a dancelike ritual where penguins huddle in a circle formation and rotate to change positions. Students are put into groups of ten and tasked with figuring out a pattern, or way to work together, to share the center of the circle (which would equate with warmth for penguins). They are challenged to do this in the most effective and timely way. Essentially, the challenge is to see what pattern of movement they can invent to accomplish this task in the quickest amount of time. Students begin to work diligently, trying out different ideas, sharing leadership, and giving and taking of ideas. At the end of about 5–10 minutes, groups share what they devised and each of the groups are timed. It is always fascinating to see how the groups work together to accomplish this task and how each group often comes up with a different solution.
  - *Schools of fish:* The next challenge is to work as a school of fish. You can show a short clip from the Disney film *Finding Nemo*, where the fish come together to make funny pictures of a big scary fish or pirate ship. Next, place students in groups of six, and ask them to come up with a way to move together as a group in the most effective and efficient way without talking. As music is played, these newly formed schools of fish work to move around the space and each other demonstrating their ideas for solving the problem. Some groups choose to make a line, some make a triangle shape linked with one hand on each shoulder for ease of picking up cues from the leader, some groups devise hand

motions to signal a move to the right or left. In all cases, students are moving, thinking, talking about the subject, and collaborating to problem solve.

- *Flocking geese*: In the last exploration, you can show a short clip of Canadian Geese flocking, how one goose takes the lead in a V formation and moves to the back of the line once it has gotten tired while another goose takes over leadership. To explore this, the entire class is asked to make a V formation with one student at the point and in the lead. The leader does a move and all other students must mimic that move. Once the leader has finished their turn, they go to the end of one of the lines and a new leader takes the front. Students also learn that the geese encourage each other when in flight by honking and supporting their fellow geese in their leadership role. To mimic this, students are asked to give a cheer or clap as each leader completes their role at the point of our V (see *flocking* lesson plan at the end of this chapter).

- *Elaborate*: After all of these experiences have been completed, students are asked to reflect on the question: in what ways did these animal groups work together to survive, and the list of ideas from students is often extensive:
  - Sharing leadership
  - Taking turns
  - Encouraging each other
  - Working together
- *Evaluate:* Ask students to reflect on their experience working together to accomplish the three challenges. In what ways did they act in ways similar to these animal groups to be successful in their challenges. In what ways did they: share leadership, take turns, encourage each other, and work together, and what was the result? You may also include an exit ticket to evaluate students, asking them to explain interdependence in animals, giving an example of how this is accomplished using one of the activities they explored in this lesson.

This example is meant to provide a more in-depth description of how one can integrate movement into a science lesson, which is driven by inquiry, allows for student exploration of a question, and the processing and reflecting on learning at the end. There are many ways that movement and theater can be used to enrich and deepen the learning in your science classroom. Consider the following ideas for "acting" out scientific concepts as well as lesson plans provided at the end of this chapter.

"Acting" Out Scientific Concepts

As was discussed in the chapter on integrating movement and theater with mathematics, having students explore complex concepts using movement is helpful for student understanding and retention (see Figure 7.3). Science learning also has a lot of complex concepts that can be challenging for students to visualize. Having students act out these ideas using movement can make these ideas more concrete (Glenberg, 2014). Here are some scientific concepts that can be explored through movement:

Centrifugal force: Take a scooter (most PE teachers have these) and a rope, offer students a chance to be swung in a circular motion to feel centrifugal

Figure 7.3 Preservice teachers in course integrating the arts across the curriculum demonstrate how the Earth rotates around the Sun

(Photograph taken by author with permission from students)

force first hand. Ask students about what might happen if you change the length of the rope. Next, ask students to get into groups to explore different ways that they can create centrifugal force; share with the group and discuss.

Types of gravity: (the moon walk): Help students understand how different types of gravity effect motion. Ask students to walk around the room normally as you explain the type of gravitational pull that is on the earth. Explain that there is a different form of gravity on the moon. Ask them to mimic this by imagining that they are skipping across a pond leaping from one stepping stone to the other. This motion (and feeling of levity) mimics what an astronaut would look like walking on the moon due to the change of gravity. After exploring, show a video of an astronaut walking on the moon.

Exploring cycles: Explore the ideas of cycles (plant cycle, life cycles) using the format of **diamonds** (see lesson plan in Chapter 3). Provide students with some source for content, either book, slides, or cards. Ask them to find motions to represent each stage of a cycle and use the *diamonds* exercise to perform the cycle for the class. As groups perform, ask observing students to identify aspects of the cycles they notice using specific scientific terms.

Open and closed circuits: Have students stand in a circle and hold hands. Ask one student to "pass the pulse," which means that they gently squeeze the hand of the person next to them. As they gain the energy, they pass the energy on to the next student by squeezing the next student's hand. This passes the "squeeze" or energy around the circle. Explain this is a closed circuit. Have two students let go of their hands and try again. The energy stops where the circle has a gap, which can explain an open circuit. (Share that this is a common activity actors do before a performance to get excited for the show!) Build upon this engineering lesson by making a *human machine* (see Box 7.4).

Model of a cell or atom: Have students create a human model of an atom or cell. Put students into groups of 3 or 4. Provide a visual for a cell and ask them to use their bodies to demonstrate how a cell functions.

Staging the water cycle: Show a visual model of the water cycle. Put students in groups of 4–5 and have them find a way to physicalize (demonstrate the water cycle.) Share final work with the whole class. Not only are the students learning by doing, but they will learn greatly from seeing the work of their

> **Human Machine**
>
> Have students explore the idea of a machine and how parts work together to accomplish a task. Ask students to work in groups of five with each student making a motion that builds off the motion of the previous student; help them understand how each must relate in some way to the previous motion, imagining if they were moving one object (even water) from the start of the machine to the end. Next, explain the types of simple machines. Have students work in groups of three to create a human model of a simple machine that uses one of six types: pulley, wheel and axle, inclined plane, wedge, and screw.

Box 7.4 Human Machine Activity

peers. This allows them to more fully process the concepts of the water cycle and use scientific terms while they identify the variety of ways that students demonstrate precipitation, condensation, evaporation, and collection.

SCIENCE IN MOTION LESSON PLANS

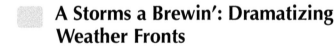

A Storms a Brewin': Dramatizing Weather Fronts

Grades 1–6

Want students to experience first-hand what happens when cold and warm air meet and battle it out? Have them work in groups to develop a way to dramatize what happens when a front is created. In this lesson, structures are provided to help guide students to summarize key facts and develop their own way of performing the information. This structure could be used for a variety of lessons, particularly concepts that contain a process or transformation.

What You Need

- Open space
- Chart paper and board

- Some medium for content about weather fronts (video clip, website access, or reading)

Student Learning Objective

Students generate ideas for choreography based on the study of weather patterns, and in doing so, model the ways that atmospheres interact to create weather fronts.

How to Do the Activity

1. Read a short explanation and/or watch a short film clip about weather fronts and what happens when warm and cold air meet or give groups of students a weather front to research. Be sure to include information on the four different front patterns: cold front, warm front, stationary front, and occluded front.
2. Place students in groups of 4–5 to create a movement piece that models one of the 4 front patterns.
3. Share first "draft" of movement piece with the class. Each group should share their piece asking observers to describe what they are seeing—making connections to scientific terminology. For example, "when you moved in a circle, were you modeling how an air front moves?"
4. Offer feedback to move the work forward: Possible questions to ask students:
   - Do you think the audience will understand what you are showing here? If not, how can you make it more clear?
   - How can you show versus tell what is happening in this front?
   - Are all members being heard? Have you tried out a variety of ideas?
5. Share final work.

Reflect and Wrap Up

- Discuss and chart similarities and differences in the fronts.
- Discuss what ways in which using movement helped to illuminate the process.
- Ask students to share how different groups articulated the same idea— were they similar or different? What was the impact of those decisions on the end product? How did that impact understanding of the concepts?

Extension/Adaptations

This process can be adapted to any study of weather patterns; simply adjust the content and adapt to the grade level and abilities of the group. This format can be adapted to learn most scientific processes.

Standards Addressed

NCAS. Dance. DA:Cr1.1.4 a. Identify ideas for choreography generated from a variety of stimuli (for example, music/sound, text, objects, images, notation, observed dance, and experiences).

NGSS. 5-ESS2-1 Earth's Systems. Develop a model using an example to describe ways the geosphere, biosphere, hydrosphere, and/or atmosphere interact.

Flocking

Grades K-6

Birds of a feather really do flock together. This is a fun and active activity that has students play a follow the leader type game that can be used in any grade to support a unit on animals or to improve focus and class cohesion (by practicing sharing leadership).

What You Need

- Open space
- Music

Student Learning Objective

Students work together to explore and explain how and why animals form groups to survive and what ways they work together to do so.

How to Do the Activity

1. Ask students why there is the saying "birds of a feather flock together?" List some possible reasons for why animals travel in packs.
2. Show a video on geese flying south for the winter and the unusual V formation that they make. Ask students to notice and provide some thoughts about what they see and what might be the reasons

for this formation. Check out this YouTube video on geese flying in their V formation: http://youtu.be/8tz1IgB6IeA

3. Asks students to make a V formation with one person at the point and two lines of students leading up to that point. (You can also do this activity in groups of 8 or 10).

4. The student at the point of the V will be the leader. They will move their arms in any way they want. (It is best to begin just with arms so that the whole group can follow along and all move as if one. It is also helpful to encourage students to move slowly. If the leader moves too fast, it is tricky for the other students to follow them.) Picking a slow music helps with this goal.

5. When the leader is tired (and feels done), they will move to the back of one of the lines, and without talking a new leader will move to the front of the V.

6. Ask students to give a sign of approval after each leader has finished like a quick clap, cheer, or words of encouragement: "way to go!"

7. Repeat until all students have had a chance to take the lead

8. Explain that geese flock and fly in a special formation of a V, which allows the whole group to be more efficient. The group of geese help and encourage each other on the long journey to warmer climate. When the leader is flying, the other geese make noises to cheer them on. When they are tired, they go to the back and another bird takes on the leadership role.

Reflect and Wrap Up

- What ways do geese work together to survive?
- How was this similar or different to other ways animals work together to survive?
- What helped you work together to accomplish the task of the lesson? Any similarities to how these geese worked together?

Standards Addressed

NCAS. DANCE. DA:Cr2.1.PK. b. Engage in dance experiences moving alone or with a partner.

NGSS.3-LS2-1. Ecosystems: Interactions, Energy, and Dynamics. Construct an argument that some animals form groups that help members survive.

Force and Motion: Types of Force

Grades 4–6

This activity will allow your students to explore the different types of force (push, pull, drag, lift, etc.) using their bodies and experience the difference between balanced and unbalanced force.

What You Need

- A large open space with a smooth floor like school gym (no carpet)
- Music

Student Learning Objective

Students will identify types of force and conduct an investigation to provide evidence of the effects that unbalanced forces have on the motion of an object and in doing so demonstrate a range of locomotor movement and directionality.

How to Do the Activity

1. Brainstorm a list of all the types of force that students can imagine.
2. Pair students (about the same size).
3. Explore balanced force: Ask the pairs to stand facing each other, put their hands in the air and go palm to palm. Have them work to find complete balance so that they are practically holding each other up. (When it doesn't work and they can't find balance, explain that this is unbalanced force).
4. Explore more unbalanced force: Forming lines on one side of the room. (Explain this is the way that dancers "cross the floor" to practice new steps.) Make three or four rows (students are together in their row).
5. Remind students of their agreement to be safe with each other's bodies taking great care when moving their partner.
6. Call out a type of force such as "push" and the students will find a way to demonstrate this concept with their partner as they cross the floor.
7. The front pair in each line will go first and cross the floor (about half way) before you call the second set of pairs in line, and so on. The pairs will cross the floor and make a new line on the other side

of the classroom waiting for all the pairs to finish. Then they turn around and prepare to cross back with new moves.

8. Remind the students that you are looking for varied and imaginative ways to move and that they should attempt to be unique in their choices.

9. Continue until you have explored a variety of forces: push, pull, drag, slide, etc.

10. Change partners; ask students if it is easier or more challenging to move different students' bodies—discuss the role of different types of clothing in effort to discuss friction.

Extension

Create a dance piece called "force and motion" by combining students' movements and putting them into a pattern that works as a dance.

Reflect and Wrap Up

• Define balanced and unbalanced forces: how did that "play" out in the performed movements?

• What were the results of changing partners and how did that affect movement? What could be the causes of those differences? (Discuss friction.)

• Did moving the body help you explore these ideas? How many types of force can they list now?

Standards Addressed

NCAS. DA:Pr5.1.1 a. Demonstrate a range of locomotor and non-locomotor movements, body patterning, body shapes, and directionality.

NGSS. 3-PS2-1 Motion and stability: Forces and interactions. Plan and conduct an investigation to provide evidence of the effects of balanced and unbalanced forces on the motion of an object.

Protons, Neutrons, and Atoms: *Do opposites really attract?*

Grades 4–6

In this active and fun lesson, students will explore various activities to help them discover how neutrons, protons, and electrons behave inside an atom. Students will act as neutrons and electrons and practice attracting and repelling their counterparts. Students will also work together to create a model of an atom.

What You Need

- An open space
- Music

Student Learning Objective

Students will choose movements that express the idea of negative, positive, and neutral charges and work together to develop a model to demonstrate the atomic composition.

How to Do the Activity

Part 1: Opposites attract

1. Explain the main parts of an atom and the function of the proton, neutron, and electron. Great video for kids explaining atoms and molecules: http://youtu.be/R1RMV5qhwyE
2. Ask students to find a space in the room where they can move their body safely without bumping into another student. Ask them to use their body to demonstrate: a neutron (and what having no charge or a neutral charge could look like in the body), next use the body to show a positive charge (proton) and a negative charge (electron).
3. Assign students to be either a proton or electron (1/2 of each). Explain that since protons have a positive charge, they will have a positive physicality (using ideas generated in the first step). They might smile, eyes bright and welcoming, or have arms extended. The other half of the students who have been assigned to electrons, will have a negative charge, therefore their bodies will have a negative physicality. They might cross their arms, eyes averted, and an angry or unwelcoming facial expression.
4. Explain that when the music plays, they must move safely around the room.
5. As students move around the room (set a pace—either slow motion, quick, medium speeds, etc.). It would be good to start with slow motion. Tell students that as they move around the

room, they need to react to each "person" they come in contact with. If they are a neutron and then come in contact with another neutron—what would happen? What would we see? (They must move toward each other and then repel.) If two electrons come close, what will they do? (They will also repel.) If an electron and a neutron come in contact with each other they will attract and stay together.

6. When the music stops, they must find their match.

Part 2: Creating an atom

Students work in groups of five or six to create a human model of an atom, share with the group as there may be multiple ways to enact this.

Extension/Adaptation

• See electron/proton greeting (*particles greeting*, Box 7.2).
• Have students work in groups of 4–6 to create a dance piece that explores positive, negative, and neutral charges and magnetic attraction

Reflect and Wrap Up

After each group performs, ask: how did this group choose to depict an atom or how are they depicting the electron's path, etc.

Standards Addressed

NGSS. MS-PS1 Matter and its interactions. Develop models to describe the atomic composition of simple molecules and extended structures.

NCAS. DA:Cr2.1.2b. Choose movements that express a main idea or emotion, or follow a musical phrase. Explain reasons for movement choices.

The Journey of a Monarch Butterfly, A Dramatization

Grades 3–5

There isn't a more dramatic story out there that compares with the migration of a Monarch Butterfly. They travel great lengths to get to their breeding grounds against all odds and they make the journey not for themselves but for the next generation of butterflies. This lesson encourages students to take this story and create a dramatization that brings the story with all its emotions to the "stage" in effort for them to understand the process more fully and to teach others about what they have learned.

What You Need

- Open space
- Picture book with facts about the Monarch Butterflies

Student Learning Objective

Students will create roles, imagined worlds, and improvised stories in a dramatic work in effort to dramatize the life cycle of the Monarch Butterfly and compare it to other animals' life cycles.

How to Do the Activity

1. Before doing this lesson, it would be helpful to do some basic improvisation lessons with your students so they have the skills to do this activity effectively (see "Improvisation 101" in Chapter 3).
2. Start this lesson with a question: What do students know about Monarch Butterflies? Tell them they will create a play to share the dramatic story with their school community and help teach others about the journey of the Monarch Butterfly.
3. Allow time for research. This can take the mode of a read aloud or offering books, websites, and handouts that share the basic facts about the life cycle and migration pattern of a Monarch Butterfly.
4. Put students in groups of four or five.
5. Ask them to discuss a possible way to tell this story through drama. Perhaps they want to do a puppet show, a dance, a mimed piece with a storyteller, or bring it to life in a play where even the butterflies can talk.
6. Give students this structure to help them get started:
   - Decide on a format to start: dance, puppet show, dramatization, and how the story will be told (narrator, characters speak, combination of the two).
   - Assign roles: Have students agree on the who, what, and where (see "Improvisation 101": *Establishing the who, what, where* in Chapter 3.)

7. Give students time to work. The process of improvising a play is about play. It's about trying out a few things and seeing what works and doesn't work and moving on from there.
8. Share work. This is an important part of the process. Students will see what works and doesn't work by gauging the response from their classmates. They will also see some exemplars which will push them to improve their work.
9. Revise and rework. Give students time to revise work and make necessary adjustments based on the feedback they receive.

Helpful Hints

Suggest students use personification in this process, allowing their butterflies to talk and tell their story. Encourage students to think outside the box—maybe their format is a talk show and they are interviewing butterflies that have made this journey—or a newscast capturing the story. The journey of the butterfly includes some special places that have unique music and cultural traditions. These could be woven into their dramatization.

Reflect and Wrap Up

- What did students learn about the life cycle of a monarch butterfly?
- Why might creating a dramatization be a helpful way to share this story?
- In what ways is the life cycle of a Monarch Butterfly similar or different to other life cycles.

Adaptation/Extension

Making Students Experts: Students could be put into groups and each group given a different migration story to research and dramatize. At the end of the "unit,' each group shares their work. Students are then able to see the varied life cycles and migration stories of different animals which they can compare and contrast.

Social Studies: Have students create a map of the path of the migration of the Monarch Butterfly.

For younger students: You can narrate the story allowing them all to act as monarch butterflies and they "act out" each stage of the process.

Standards Addressed

NGSS. 3-LS1-1. From molecules to organisms: Structures and processes. Develop models to describe that organisms have unique and diverse life cycles but all have in common birth, growth, reproduction, and death.

NCAS. Theater. TH:Cr1.1.3. a. Create roles, imagined worlds, and improvised stories in a drama/theatre work.

The Solar System: *Dancing Through Space*

In this group of exercises, your students will experience different types of motions found in space. They will move like the sun, moon, and planets, using their bodies and balloons to explore how the sun, moon, and earth relate to each other to create night/day and the seasons on Earth.

What You Need

- An open space to work, preferably on a smooth surface without rugs
- Music: (Classical works well)
- Optional: colored balls or balloons

Student Learning Objective

Students demonstrate and describe patterns of Sun, Moon, and Earth and its impact on night/day and seasons while building content for choreography using the stimuli of a natural phenomenon.

How to Do the Activity (Note: Music should be used throughout this lesson)

Part 1: Exploring motions in space

Write on the board a group of terms that will be explored through movement in the following exercise: rotation, revolution, orbit, elliptical orbit, axis, clockwise, and counterclockwise. Tell students they will do the work of dancers and use their bodies to explore these types of movements:

Axis & rotation: Define Axis and rotation. Concept to explore: The earth rotates on its "imaginary" axis. Cross the floor exercise: Have students cross the floor (you can do multiple lines with the first person in each line going together and after a few moments, the next in line go). Using their strongest leg as an axis allowing their body to be the earth, have student cross the floor, stepping forward, and turning on their leg as they move across the room. Dancers call this a pirouette. They should repeat this move as they cross the floor allowing for a few steps in between each pirouette.

Orbit: Put students in pairs to explore the concept of orbit (a gravitationally curved path of an object around a point in space). Have each pair spend a few minutes exploring all the different ways they can orbit each other. Ask each pair to share their favorite example at the end of the exercise.

Elliptical orbit—The earth orbits the sun and revolution: With the same or different partner, ask the pairs to explore and be prepared to demonstrate how the earth orbits the sun. Remind students of what they know (or have discussed) about how the earth and the sun move. Encourage them to find their own unique way to demonstrate this orbit. It is fun to use plastic balls (or colored balloons) to represent the sun and earth or the children can use their bodies (see Figure 7.3). Explain that the earth does not make a perfect circle around the sun but moves in an elliptical or egg-like-shaped fashion. Use the term revolution to describe one full circle of the earth around the sun.

Clockwise and counterclockwise: The earth and the moon both orbit in a counterclockwise way. Work with a pair to demonstrate three different ways to move in a clockwise and counterclockwise way.

Synchronous rotation: The moon has a unique way of moving with the earth. This is called a synchronous rotation. To explore this rotation, have students hold each other's right hands, so that each child will be facing the opposite direction. Have students completely extend their arms and rotate balancing their weight with their partner. This demonstrates how the moon's relationship to the earth in motion is very different from the earth and sun's relationship in motion.

Part 2: Application of lessons: Write two questions on the board. Ask students to work in groups of three to demonstrate the answer to the following questions:

1. What explains for the fact that the sun rises in the east and sets in the west? How would the earth move itself and around the sun to make this happen?
2. How would the earth need to orbit the sun in effort to explain for the change of seasons? (Have students use a sticker or tape to mark one side of the ball so that this can be more easily demonstrated.)

Adaptations/Extensions

Extension: Have students work in groups of three to demonstrate the more complex movement relationship between earth, moon, and sun.

Perform: Create a group dance performance by piecing together the various outcomes of each of these exercises. Use a screen that has the terms projected on the board allowing various groups to perform: having solos, duets, trios, and whole class, building one after the other until you have a complete piece.

Standards Addressed

NGSS. 1-ESS1-1. Use observations of the sun, moon, and stars to describe patterns that can be predicted. Core Ideas: ESS1.A: The universe and its stars: Patterns of the motion of the sun, moon, and stars in the sky can be observed, described, and predicted. Season patterns of sunrise and sunset can be observed, described, and predicted.

5-ESS1-2. Represent data in graphical displays to reveal patterns of changes in length and direction of shadows, day and night, and seasonal appearance of some stars in the night sky.

NCAS. Dance. DA:Cr1.1.5 a. Build content for choreography using several stimuli (for example, music/sound, text, objects, images, notation, observed dance, experiences, literary forms, natural phenomena, current news, and social events).

References

Burnaford, G., Aprill, A., & Weiss, C. (2001). *Renaissance in the classroom: Arts integration and meaningful learning.* Lawrence Erlbaum Associates, Inc.

Glenberg, A. (2014). How acting out in schools boosts learning. *Scientific American.* http://www.scientificamerican.com/article/how-acting-out-in-school-boosts-learning/

Goldberg, M. (2021). *Arts integration: Teaching subject matter through the arts in multicultural settings* (6th ed.). Routledge.

Hardiman, M., JohnBull, R. M., Carran, D. T., & Shelton, A. (2019). The effects of arts-integrated instruction on memory for science content. Trends in Neuroscience and Education, 14, 25–32.

Johnson-Glenberg, M. C., Birchfield, D. A., Tolentino, L., & Koziupa, T. (2014). Collaborative embodied learning in mixed reality motion-capture environments: Two science studies. *Journal of Educational Psychology, 106*(1), 86–104. https://doi.org/10.1037/a0034008

Roth, W. M. (2001). Gestures: Their role in teaching and learning. *Review of Education Research, 71*(3), 365–392. https://doi-org.ezproxy.uvm.edu/10.3102/00346543071003365

Tonelli, F. (2013). Science as ground of the Renaissance artists. *Clinical Cases in Mineral and Bone Metabolism, 10*(1), 68–69. https://doi.org/10.11138/ccmbm/2013.10.1.068

8 Moving Toward Authentic Assessments Using the Arts

Picture This...

I am teaching my arts integration class for college-age students and soon to be elementary school teachers. We have just finished the lesson that was just described in the science in motion chapter where students worked in groups to explore through movement the varied ways that animals work together to survive. The students began by exploring the ways that penguins huddle to stay warm, working as a team to figure out the quickest and most efficient pattern of movement to ensure each "penguin" gets some time in the warm center. Next, they worked as a school of fish to enact the most effective way to move as one navigating the other groups through our classroom. Finally, students acted as a flock of geese with one student in the leadership role and all others mimicking their chosen move. As each leader tires, they move to the end of the V formation allowing another student to take the lead, which teaches students how a flock shares leadership in effort to travel great distances. After all this physical activity, exploration of concepts, sharing of work, and offering observations, we process the lesson. I ask students to offer up examples of ways that animals work together to survive. Students begin to recount the various ways they experienced this during the lesson: shared leadership, communication, working as a team, coming together in a larger group for safety. Then one student raises his hand and in a combination of question and comment offers: "This was a cool activity and everything, but how do you transition from

DOI: 10.4324/9781003296317-8

this fun stuff to making sure students really learned something?" I could read between the lines on this one. In a way he was commenting on the entire process and was seeing all this exploration as outside of the learning. He was expressing his concern about moving from the "fun stuff" back to "real" science class and the impact this might have on student learning. I explained that assessment was happening throughout the lesson as I observed students work to solve the challenges while discussing the content, as I guided them through each stage of the activity by asking driving questions, and as I reflected with them at the end of the lesson. He didn't seem convinced. I went on to explain that there was no reason you couldn't combine arts integration lessons with more traditional assessments. I suggested that at the end of this lesson, a teacher could easily provide an exit ticket to assess each student's understanding of the content. This seemed to assuage him. It was a good learning lesson for me to remember that the way we do school and have done school has a long history and that breaking away from that tradition can make people feel uncomfortable and unsure. It was helpful to explain to this student that the "fun" part in the middle of the lesson was our exploration time, like doing a science experiment, field trip, or math game. The important step is to process the experience at the end with students to help them make sense of all they experienced and transition that into learning.

Offering this student a middle ground for assessing arts integrated lessons is one avenue for creating a bridge between a non-traditional learning experience (using the arts as a vehicle for learning and exploring a concept) and a more traditional one (a science class that has an exit ticket at the end to check for learning gains). However, this chapter will also explore the notion that using the arts in your classroom, specific-ally dance and theater, provides a new lens for assessing students' pro-gress that might not be captured in more traditional assessment forms that rely heavily on writing or test taking. In the arts integrated science lesson described, students were able to share their learning in a variety of ways, from physically demonstrating a concept to vocalizing their understanding while working to create their movement demonstrations. In this way, the arts were not only a vehicle for learning, but a vehicle for authentic assessment that provided information about where students are at in their learning process.

The Benefits of Art Making for Assessment

Burnaford et al. (2001) who began the Chicago Arts Partnership in Education (CAPE), one of the most successful arts programs in the country, describe the role of assessment in an arts integrated unit:

> [It] involves exhibition and performance perhaps in conjunction with traditional testing. It incorporates self-evaluation, the design of rubrics, and the involvement of students in establishing standards of quality. It centers on thoughtful reflection- not just at the end when the product is unveiled, but at each step along the way. The process of assessment is as integrative as the art projects.
>
> (p. 90)

These art educators offer a multitude of ideas to consider when assessing arts integrated lessons including combining art making with a more traditional assessment form like a test. They also emphasize the importance of self-reflection and the inclusion of the student in the assessment process. This aligns well with current trends in education that encourage students to be more involved in their own learning (such as with personal learning plans, PLPs). Another key take away from this excerpt is the importance of assessment throughout the process, as a means to guide the learner, but also the teacher providing evidence about adjustments needed to insure optimal learning.

While the activities and lesson plans provided in this book could be combined with a more traditional form of assessment (checklist, exit ticket, written response, quiz), using the art-making process as a way to explore content and then using a more traditional form of an assessment to check for understanding of the content, it misses a key benefit of using the arts in the assessment process. When engaging students in making art and using the body as a mode for learning, students have varied ways to show what they know. These processes may provide better avenues for seeing where students are at and for some students to demonstrate their thinking in other ways; which may be more conducive to their level and abilities. Such practices are particularly effective for students who may struggle with writing or be EL learners (Fattal, 2019).

Think back to the story shared about the two young students who came alive during a social studies lesson that integrated theater into a study of

Westward Expansion. They were tasked with creating skits about packing the wagon to travel on the Oregon Trail. They took on leadership, collaborated with their peers to perform a scene, and shared many facts learned from the readings in their performance. These students also demonstrated more engagement than was typical for them, which may have provided more opportunity to evaluate what they know. This increase in both engagement and in opportunities to share thinking was experienced by the majority of the class as expressed by their classroom teacher who was surprised about how much all the students could recall from their readings when using playbuilding as a mode for learning.

What might explain this phenomenon, that students performing scenes about their learning in social studies could result in a more comprehensive assessment of where students are at? One explanation is that integrating theater and movement into classroom instruction increases engagement (Smithrim & Upitis, 2005). Theater activities often feel more fun to kids, so they are more willing to get involved (Sawyer, 2004). Increased student engagement in both the learning process and in the sharing of what they know can result in stronger assessment data (Goldberg, 2021). Additionally, such activities are novel, and novelty can impact student engagement and learning (Hardiman, 2012). Novelty signals the brain that something new is happening and that it's time to be alert. How often do we ask students to write an essay or a response to questions, and they give us that look that signals, "really, this again?" Providing a different way to capture students' thinking and learning may provide more insights into their understanding because the assessment is actually something they want to participate in.

Theater making also provides an opportunity for students to share what they learned in a different way which may help us to better evaluate where our students are at in their learning, especially our struggling students. Think back to the first story in this book about the young man who raised his fist in the air when I referenced Martin Luther King and the Civil Rights Movement. He was sharing in some small (but not insignifi-cant) way his connection with and retention of the content. Creating new and varied ways to assess student learning will ensure that all students succeed because they are able to share what they have learned in a way that might work better for them. If we only rely on forms of assessment that heavily depend on writing skills, we may be assessing the skill of writing more than gauging what students know and understand about the content. While the skill of writing is an essential skill and should be developed and encouraged across the curriculum, relying solely on this form of communication can be limiting. As Fattal (2019) has argued, if we only rely on the written and spoken word to assess student learning, we are leaving out a large majority of our student population, especially students who are ELs. Albers (2006) affirms the importance of a multimodal approach for curriculum design and assessment in literacy as it offers more flexibility and choice for how students express their learning.

The arts can also provide a lens into students' abilities that may not be "showing up" in traditional methods. Goldberg (2021) calls this "incidental assessment," which she explains occurs when a child is engaged in art making and demonstrates abilities beyond the art making that lead you to a more complete picture of their overall development (not necessarily just in the subject area). When conducting a unit on drumming with a group of fourth graders a few years back, one student really stood out, engaging in the learning unlike anything I had seen of him in the classroom so far. When his parents came in for the parents' conference, they were very focused on their child's progress in math and science. I shared what I had witnessed during these drumming lessons that revealed some skills and talents this student possessed that had not been observed prior like leadership and spatial awareness. He also just came alive! This student was not excelling in math as his parents had hoped, but in the drumming lessons, he was head of the class. I saw a leader, a creative problem solver, and a collaborator who picked up on cues and was able to make changes as necessary to move the process forward. He demonstrated skills that could lead someone to becoming a CEO or entrepreneur. One of the most powerful reasons for arts in classrooms is that when students engage in these practices, students who often struggle in more traditional modes of learning, shine brightly. This improves self-esteem that often leads to more success in other subjects as well (Goldberg, 2021).

Becoming a Connoisseur or Curator: Viewing Assessment with an Artistic Lens

In the age of high stakes testing and accountability, assessment can too often be thought of as the end game—what did students learn and how can that learning most efficiently be evaluated. This is often deemed assessment "of" learning versus assessment "for" learning. Assessment of learning often leads to more traditional modes of assessment like tests, quizzes, and written responses that are more easily quantified. However, Burnaford et al. (2001) remind us that the origin of the term assessment comes from the French word, *assidere*, which means to "sit beside" (p. 89). Sitting beside children implies listening, observing, and watching. It is a process of collecting data that informs us where students are at so we can move them forward. Using arts in the assessment process provides an opportunity to observe, see, and hear students as they are more active in their learning. It provides what the anthropologist, Clifford Geertz, calls "thick description," a more complete and rich picture of where students are at in their learning process that is informative and useful not only about the students' learning but as a means to inform our instruction and next steps in the learning cycle (Burnaford et al.,2001).

Capturing and evaluating thick description in classrooms requires what Elliot Eisner (2002) describes as *connoisseurship* (p. 189). This term, which has traditionally been used to describe art critics who appreciate and evaluate works in the visual arts, may provide educators with a new way of thinking about and conducting assessments. Connoisseurship, as defined by Eisner (2002), is the "art of appreciation" (p. 187). A connoisseur has developed their ability to see what others do not and to know what they are looking at. Thinking of oneself as a connoisseur expands what one might consider as an evaluator or assessor: "It is intended to avoid the radical reductionism that characterizes much of quantitative description. It is designed to provide a fine- grained picture of what has occurred or has been accomplished so that practice or policy can be improved and high quality of achievement acknowledge" (Eisner, 2002, p. 189).

Making what is seen and experienced visual requires what Eisner calls *educational criticism* and includes four features:

- *Describe*: The critic must describe student work in vivid detail so it captures what is seen so when they share it, others can imagine it.
- *Interpret*: The critic must account for what they have described, to explain why and how they have described it as such, making a connection to the context in which this description has been captured.
- *Evaluate:* The critic must then make some judgment of what they are seeing, which is more expansive than a simple value given: "meets," "exceeds," or "progressing"—it involves considering the quality of work and the growth of the student's development. It considers the

quality of student engagement, and if they are meaningfully involved in the activities.

- *Thematize*: Critics take what they learn from these three stages to make big picture conclusions that may impact other learning in the classroom for our students as well as our own practice.

Thinking of oneself as a connoisseur may offer an opportunity to expand your assessment practice to be more inclusive and provide more meaningful information for both you and your students, helping you to better capture how your students are progressing as well as finding ways to impact the quality of learning in your classroom.

Donovan and Anderberg (2020) suggest that educators think of themselves as "curators." A curator is a person who is responsible for the collection and presentation of artifacts in a museum. Using this lens, the job of the educator is to collect evidence or "documentation" that helps develop a narrative that points to growth and further learning. Documentation of evidence is a key aspect of this approach and utilizes concepts of the "Making Learning Visible" framework created by Project Zero, a research arm of the Harvard's School of Education. The framework suggests that documentation involves a specific question that guides the process, includes collecting and interpreting of observations, makes use of multiple languages (or ways to represent thinking), makes learning visible, and is prospective (shapes the design for future learning) (Donovan & Anderberg, 2020; Making Learning Visible, 2005). Whether you take on the role of connoisseur or curator, let the arts help you re-envision your assessment practice.

Authentic Assessment and the Arts

One of the strongest arguments for including arts in your assessment practices is that it provides an opportunity for authentic assessment. Authentic assessments are tasks, projects, or problem-solving challenges that mirror real life challenges in various disciplines (Wilbert, 2013). When engaging in arts integrated projects like the ones presented in this book, you are providing an opportunity for authentic assessment because the product of their creative process is a real-world creation: a play, scene, dance, or presentation. It may also be an outcome of working as a team to solve a challenge presented in class like using the body to create a model of the water cycle or figuring out the best way to move as a group through the classroom as a school of fish. When students take content learned from readings or classroom instruction and make something with it, they are also reaching the highest level of Bloom's taxonomy which is *create*. These authentic assessments can provide educators with lots of information about where students are at with their learning, how they are making sense of the content, and even how much they are retaining. It can also provide insights into what areas they did not understand as well.

Evaluating Authentic Assessments

The next step is to gather evidence of student learning to process what you have seen, heard, and observed into a format that provides insights for both you and your students. Evaluating authentic assessments can take many forms: observation notes, rubrics, check lists, and self-assessments.

Formative Assessment

Since evaluating arts integrated projects or processes (outcomes of the day's tasks) may be new for you, rest assured that assessment in any content area follows a similar format and is grounded in defining what students can show they can do by the end of the lesson or unit. However, when engaging in arts integrated projects, the formative assessment process, or assessment *for* learning, is paramount. Often projects take some time to develop and the key to success is guiding the student through the process offering quality feedback that can move them forward. It is a checkpoint: where are my students right now and what can I do to help them progress toward deeper learning and a high-quality product?

The Kennedy Center, a leader in arts integration, offers a process for formative assessments for arts integrated lessons which includes four parts:

- *Establish criteria*: What do we want students to learn, what are our learning goals, and what does it look like when our students meet them. These established criteria articulate these goals to our students. They can be in the form of a checklist or rubric.

- *Observe*: This is where we collect data by looking at what students: do, say, create. We observe how students are engaging with the content, listen to their conversations about the content (having informal check ins as needed to redirect, clarify, or ask driving questions).
- *Clarify*: As we observe student work, either during the process (art making) or the sharing of work, we offer feedback either through questions or direct feedback and make suggestions for further exploration. We share our observations in relation to the learning goals.
- *Direct*: In this stage, we either move them forward to the next stage or send them back for more revision, rehearsal or investigation.

Process over Product

The discussion of a formative assessment leads to an important aspect of working with the arts that is key to understanding its value in our educational landscape: the process is as important if not more than the product. In the high-stakes educational system we inhabit, getting students to the product (a documentation of what they can do) and assessing that product often takes priority. The arts can offer a new lens for thinking about learning and the importance of process as well as product. As Goldberg (2021) has argued, the product only gives us a small insight into our students' learning gains; the process of making art is as valuable and important and gives educators an opportunity to assess growth over time (p. 240). Goldberg also reminds us not to underestimate both engagement and self-reflection in the assessment process. (See example of a *self-reflection tool* at end of chapter).

Assessing Students' Developing Skills in Artmaking

The lessons provided in this book are grounded in a framework for learning called arts integration. The goal of arts integrated lessons is to achieve learning outcomes in both the content and the arts; in the case of this book, science, social studies, math, and literacy as well as dance and theater. You could engage in these lessons by using the arts as a vehicle for learning the content only choosing to assess students' attainment of the content. However, if you want the full benefits of this framework, you will assess students' development as performing artists as well. If you are hoping to change the type of learning done in your classroom using the arts, you will want to develop your students' capacity and skills in art making. Doing so will improve all learning outcomes because as students continue to do this work, they will become more skilled at moving, dancing, theater making, collaboration, and working as a team to create a work of art which will give them the tools to more deeply engage in the learning process. They will be able to be more independent in their work, will take the level of learning to new heights, and will be making some incredible art!

Failing to assess your students' progress in the arts signals to the students that the arts are not important. As we think about assessment, the elephant in the room is—we assess what we value. If we only assess the content in these lessons, the arts are devalued. And if you signal to the students that the arts are not equally important, then they might not work to improve their skills in this arena, thereby making progress static. If you want the arts to be an equal player in your classroom, then you have to assess students' progress in attaining those skills as well as content. This entire book is meant to champion the arts and their value for schools, classrooms, students, and learning. If by the end of this book, you have discovered how valuable the arts are to learning, then you need to assess it as well.

How to Assess Students' Work in the Arts

Despite evidence that integrating the arts into classroom instruction is an effective teaching and learning strategy, many teacher education programs fail to effectively teach preservice teachers how to use the arts in their pedagogy (Hunter-Doniger & Fox, 2020). This lack of training makes assessing art making or the development of skills in an artform intimidating. Additionally, some might suggest that the assessment of the arts is not possible because there are so many varied opinions about what "good" art looks like. Goldberg (2021) debunks the myth that the arts can't be assessed because they are too subjective. She suggests three ways that all arts can be assessed:

- *Technique:* The actual skills needed to engage in the specific art form.
- *Content:* Vocabulary, history, and traditions.
- *Intellectual behaviors:* Skills needed for artmaking such as the ability to perceive, inquire, value, manipulate, and cooperate (p. 240).

Using the National Core Arts Standards as a Guide

The lesson plans provided use the *National Core Arts Standards* (NCAS) as benchmarks for the learning objectives in the arts. The NCASs are a conceptual framework for arts learning created by the National Coalition for Core Arts Standards and recognized by many states as well as leading arts organizations like The Kennedy Center for the Performing Arts. They are aligned with the four artistic processes: *creating, presenting, responding,* and *connecting.* These processes build "artistic literacy" in your students, which they define as:

> The knowledge and understanding required to participate authentically in the arts. Fluency in the language(s) of the arts is the ability to create, perform/produce/present, respond, and connect through symbolic and metaphoric forms that are unique to the arts. It is embodied in specific philosophical foundations and lifelong goals that enable an artistically literate person to transfer arts knowledge, skills, and capacities to other subjects, settings, and contexts.
>
> (NCAS, n.d., p. 17)

Why develop students' artistic literacy? Sir Ken Robinson (2006), who is deemed as a creativity expert, has argued that we are educating our students to work in future we can't even imagine. He believes that foregrounding students' skills in creativity using the arts is our best way forward to prepare our students for this unknown future. Expanding the ways we teach, embracing more creativity, can help students gain the ability to create something original that has never been done before, to see things in a new way, and to respond to something new. Artistic literacy and the ability to create, perform, respond, and connect can develop these skills in our students.

Our students are also entering a world dominated by technology where information is communicated through multimedia approaches which relies heavily on the visual and less on the written word and numeracy (*NCAS Framework*). The arts help prepare our students to contribute content in this new format, but also process, interpret, and evaluate information in this new age.

The NCAS are developed to progress students from kindergarten through high school, offering benchmarks at each stage of development. While these standards provide a helpful guide, the issue with using these standards is that not all classrooms are doing artistic work. Therefore, you might have students who are in third grade but are on the basic level in their artistic skills. The grade each skill is assigned to, therefore, is in some ways irrelevant. In a perfect world, when arts are a part of all schools' curriculum, one could move students through each stage of these benchmarks. However, in our current educational climate, where most elementary schools do not include drama and dance in their curriculum (*NCAS Framework*), it would be amiss to align your projects with the exact grade level benchmark provided by the NCAS. For this reason, the standards are used as a continuum in this book, focusing less on grade level and instead on skill level. These standards are a guide or gold standard that we are working toward with a focus on the benchmark that is most appropriate for the level of the students and their experience in artistic practices.

Key Skills That Students Need to Develop to Move Toward Proficiency in Drama and Dance Practices

How do teachers know what they are "looking at" if they have no previous experience in drama or dance? Using the NCAS as a guide, I have developed a list of key skills that can be helpful in developing your students' creative capacities and skills in the areas of theater and dance (with a guiding rubric for assessing students' development at the end of the chapter)

Key Performing Arts Skills/Competencies

> Voice expression and range
> Voice volume
> Use of body: Full body motion, use of body to tell a story (expressive)
> Listening/responding to partner and action on stage
> Imagination/creativity: demonstration of creative choices made
> Collaboration: work with others to effectively create

Additional Resources

There are so many excellent resources for creating art-based assessments, so no need to repeat here. This list provides some of the strongest models, examples, and sources for curating or creating assessments for your arts integrated lessons:

- Arts Integrated Project Rubric: Integrated PARRC assessment rubric (Riley, 2014; Robinson, 2006)

- Arts Integrated Assessment Checklist (Donovan & Anderberg, 2020, p. 177)
- Critique Assessment Worksheet (Goldberg, 2021, p. 256)
- Creating and Assessing Portfolios for Creative Processes (The Kennedy Center, 2022a, 2022b)

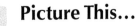 Picture This...

Your future classroom where desks are pushed to the side.

A literacy lesson where students are showing the journey of a character from their read aloud through dance.

A play performed at your school that was created by the students in your class that demonstrates all they have learned about a historical period or event.

Math class that requires no pencils.

Bodies in motion during a science lesson showing life cycles.

A classroom where children are encouraged to bring their whole selves to their learning.

Children in your classes constantly surprising you, a classroom full of laughter and students taking ownership of their own learning.

Every single class that I integrate the performing arts into a lesson, be it dance or theater, on any level, something happens that reminds me how important this work is. Just this week in my college-level class on arts integration two things stood out. I have a student who has been struggling in her core courses and sometimes has a difficult time vocalizing her thinking in class. But when we were doing a community-building activity that asked a group of students to make a human knot and then work together to untie themselves, this student amazed me. She immediately started giving directions that demonstrated her spatial awareness, ability to problem-solve and communicate, and her strength in leadership! When I gave her this positive feedback, you could tell that it meant a lot to her and her engagement in the class has skyrocketed. In another class, when visiting our university art gallery, we did a movement activity to engage with an art collection. Each of the students chose a painting and made a pose to express a movement observed in the work. A student who is very quiet in my class, and rarely contributes to class discussions, made the most powerful and moving physical move demonstrating not only how invested she was in the learning, but that she was learning and understanding the material. I was able to acknowledge this accomplishment and give her some positive reinforcement. Integrating creative movement and theater in your classroom will transform your classroom, students, and your practice. So, it's time to get *moving*!

SAMPLE ASSESSMENTS

Rubric for Assessing Competencies in the Performing Arts

	Beginning	Developing	Target
Voice expression	Student is not yet using the voice effectively to communicate ideas, voice may be monotone and lack expression	Student demonstrates some ability to use the voice to communicate ideas, is beginning to explore the range of their voice with varying outcomes, and sometimes is expressive	Student can use the voice effectively to communicate ideas: varying tone, pitch (using both the high and low register); voice is expressive and can communicates a range of emotions
Voice volume	Student's voice is quiet and not yet able to be heard by a given audience, student does not yet demonstrate an ability to vary volume for dramatic effect	Student sometimes speaks loud enough to be heard for a given audience, but often needs a reminder to speak up; they sometimes demonstrate the ability to vary their volume for dramatic effect	Student can vary their volume, using the voice quietly or loudly for dramatic effect; students can project their voice so it is heard by a given audience

(continued)

	Beginning	*Developing*	*Target*
Use of body as a communicator	Student is not yet demonstrating the use of the body to communicate ideas; student is using a small range of motion and partial use of the body	Student is beginning to use the body to communicate ideas, using some of the body and some range of motion	Student can effectively use the body to communicate ideas, using the whole body, displaying a range of motion
Listening/ responding	Student is not yet demonstrating effective listening skills and may not yet respond (or respond in line) to partner's cues	Student is demonstrating developing listening and responding skills, may vary in their abilities to respond to their partner	Student demonstrates strong listening skills by responding to their partner's cues
Creativity/ imagination	Student is not yet demonstrating the use of creativity and imagination, often mimics the ideas of others or makes choices that stay within the realm of the ideas already shared	Student is beginning to demonstrate some imagination and creativity in their choices, sporadically making a bold choice	Student demonstrates a high level of creativity and use of their imagination in their choices, making bold choices that demonstrate new and original ideas
Collaboration	Is not effectively working with a partner or a group, may struggle to take turns and/or to give and take ideas	May need some support in navigating group work or problem solving, in some cases shares ideas, but may not yet fully share or take ideas; not currently demonstrating leadership	Student works effectively with a partner or with a diverse group of students; is able to take and share ideas, demonstrating leadership, and is able to negotiate decisions in the creative process to produce an end result; demonstrates strong problem-solving skills

Self-Reflection Tool

Let's Reflect

It is vital that we reflect after we learn or experience a new idea. This helps turn this learning into a building block for other learning and transfer it to long-term memory. Take some time to reflect on our lesson today where we used the arts to learn new content.

Use this graphic organizer to reflect and organize your thoughts.

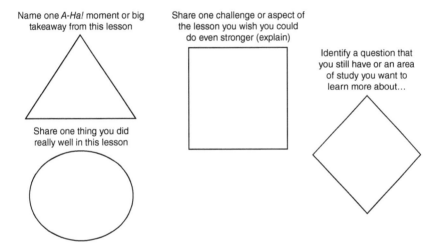

References

Albers, P. (2006). Imagining the possibilities in multimodal curriculum design. *English Education, 38*(2), 75–101. https://www.jstor.org/stable/40173215

Burnaford, G. E., Aprill, A., & Weiss, C. (Eds.). (2001). *Renaissance in the classroom: Arts integration and meaningful learning.* Lawrence Erlbaum Associates.

Donovan, L., & Anderberg, S. (2020). *Teacher as curator: Formative assessment and arts-based strategies.* Teachers College Press.

Eisner, E. W. (2002). *The arts and the creation of mind.* Yale University Press.

Fattal, L. R. (2019). Transmediational practices in a bilingual elementary classroom. *NABE Journal of Research and Practice, 9*(2), 88–95. https://doi.org/10.1080/26390043.2019.1589295

Goldberg, M. (2021). *Arts integration: Teaching subject matter through the arts in multicultural settings* (6th ed.). Routledge.

Hardiman, M. (2012). *Brain targeted teaching model for 21st-century schools*. Corwin.

Hunter-Doniger, T., & Fox, M. (2020). Arts connections: An investigation of art education course for preservice generalists. *Arts Education Policy Review, 121*(2), 55–62. https://doi.org/10.1080/10632913.2018.1530709

Kennedy Center. (2022a). *Formative assessment: Explore a process for using assessment for learning during arts integration*. Kennedy Center, Education. https://www.kennedy-center.org/education/resources-for-educators/classroom-resources/articles-and-how-tos/articles/collections/arts-integration-resources/formative-assessment/

Kennedy Center. (2022b). *Portfolios: Assessment across the arts: An introduction for arts educators to portfolio assessment*. Kennedy Center Resources for Educators. https://www.kennedy-center.org/education/resources-for-educators/classroom-resources/articles-and-how-tos/articles/educators/critique–feedback/portfolios-assessment-across-the-arts/

Making Learning Visible. (2005). Learning group and documentation: Definitions and feature one-pager. Making Learning Visible Project at the Harvard Graduate School of Education http://www.mlvpz.org/files/onepagergldoc609.pdf

National Core Arts Standards (NCAS). (n.d.). https://www.national-artsstandards.org/

Riley, S. (2014, January). *Ed closet best of 2013: Integrated PARCC assessment rubric*. Institute for Arts Integrated and STEAM. https://artsintegration.com/2014/01/02/edcloset-best-2013-integrated-parcc-assessment-rubric/

Robinson, K. (2006, June 26). *Do schools kill creativity?* [Ted Talk]. Ted Conference. https://www.ted.com/talks/sir_ken_robinson_do_schools_kill_creativity?utm_campaign=tedspread&utm_medium=referral&utm_source=tedcomshare

Sawyer, K. (2004). Creative teaching: Collaborative discussion as disciplined improvisation. *Educational Researcher, 33*(2), 12–20.

Smithrim, K., & Upitis, R. (2005). Learning through the arts: Lessons of engagement. *Canadian Journal of Education, 28*(1), 109–127.

Wilbert, M. (2013, April 19). Authentic assessment in action. *Edutopia*. https://www.edutopia.org/blog/sammamish-4-authentic-assessment-in-action-mark-wilbert

For Product Safety Concerns and Information please contact our EU
representative GPSR@taylorandfrancis.com
Taylor & Francis Verlag GmbH, Kaufingerstraße 24, 80331 München, Germany